In a Faraway Land

First published by O Books, 2010
O Books is an imprint of John Hunt Publishing Ltd., The Bothy, Deershot Lodge, Park Lane, Ropley,
Hants, SO24 0BE, UK
office1@o-books.net
www.o-books.net

Distribution in:

UK and Europe
Orca Book Services
orders@orcabookservices.co.uk
Tel: 01202 665432 Fax: 01202 666219
Int. code (44)

USA and Canada
NBN
custserv@nbnbooks.com
Tel: 1 800 462 6420 Fax: 1 800 338 4550

Australia and New Zealand
Brumby Books
sales@brumbybooks.com.au
Tel: 61 3 9761 5535 Fax: 61 3 9761 7095

Far East (offices in Singapore, Thailand,
Hong Kong, Taiwan)
Pansing Distribution Pte Ltd
kemal@pansing.com
Tel: 65 6319 9939 Fax: 65 6462 5761

South Africa
Stephan Phillips (pty) Ltd
Email: orders@stephanphillips.com
Tel: 27 21 4489839 Telefax: 27 21 4479879

Text copyright Michael Berman 2009

Design: Stuart Davies

ISBN: 978 1 84694 302 7

Printed by Digital Book Print

O Books operates a distinctive and ethical publishing philosophy in all areas of its business, from its global network of
authors to production and worldwide distribution.

In a Faraway Land

Michael Berman

BOOKS

Winchester, UK
Washington, USA

CONTENTS

A collection of traditional and contemporary tales
for classroom use, containing a comprehensive introduction
to the history and art of storytelling, detailed notes for
teachers on how to use the material with an answer key,
and photocopiable worksheets.

ACKNOWLEDGEMENTS

The photo on the front cover was taken by an artist from the Republic of Georgia, Maka Batiashvili. To see more of her work, please visit www.maka.batiashvili.net

If any copyright holders have been inadvertently overlooked, and for those copyright holders that all possible efforts have been made to contact but without success, the author will be pleased to make the necessary arrangements at the first opportunity.

STORYTELLING: AN INTRODUCTION

Storytelling is as old as humankind. Long before stories were recorded, they were entrusted to storytellers. Why did our ancestors tell stories? Historians believe storytelling was used for a number of purposes: to teach history, to settle arguments, to make sense of the world (through Creation Myths), to satisfy a need for play and entertainment, to honour supernatural forces, to communicate experiences to other humans, and to record the actions and characteristics of ancestors for future generations (through legends).

Some of the books of the Bible, such as the Song of Songs and the Book of Job, were written in dramatic storytelling form and we have documentation of storytelling from many cultures. Records of storytelling have been found in many languages, including Sanskrit, Old German, Latin, Chinese, Greek, Latin, Icelandic and Old Slavonic. The origins of storytelling, however, are even more ancient. One of our earliest surviving records is found in the Westcar Papyrus of the Egyptians, in which the sons of Cheops (the pyramid builder) entertained their father with stories. The epic tale, *Gilgamesh*, which relates the story of a Sumerian king, is frequently cited in history texts as our oldest, surviving epic tale.

Both Hinduism and Buddhism made use of storytelling for teaching purposes. Hindu storytellers used story cloths from *The Ramayana* to illustrate their narratives. *The Ramayana*, the great epic tale of India, is part of the Hindu scriptures for Rama is believed to be an incarnation of the god Vishnu. Within the Buddhist faith, Siddhartha Gautama, the founder of Buddhism, incorporated story-telling in his teachings. *The Jataka* or birth tales, are stories of previous incarnations of the Buddha. There is evidence that early Christian prophets used stories in their preaching too, but little more is known. In *Judges 9:7*, Jotham tells the people of Shechem a tale to point out the wickedness of their ruler. The Hasidic Jews also used storytelling in introducing their rituals and beliefs to young children. In the *New Testament* Jesus Christ used the parable form in his teachings. Even today, storytelling remains a part of Christian services, especially for young children and for use in Sunday Schools.

In fact, all the major religious traditions have made use of metaphorical stories to communicate their teachings - the stories from early India, Greek fables, Zen, Sufi, and Hasidic tales - as they have long been recognised as a means of bypassing the set attitudes and limitations of the conscious mind. Stories not only entertain; they can also alter our experience so as to facilitate growth and change and the stories presented in this collection have all been chosen with this aim in mind.

Why tell stories in the classroom? Because storytelling engages the imagination, promotes language development, encourages reading, teaches people about other cultures, and helps them to understand both themselves and others.

When we listen to a story the heart rate changes, the eyes dilate, the muscles contract, and in a safe way, we really do confront witches, overcome monsters, fall in love, and find our way out of dark forests. Storytelling uses the left brain's functions (language, a story line, sequences of cause and effect) to speak the right brain's language of symbolic, intuitive, imaginative truths. For example, the small bird sits on the shoulder of the boy lost in the woods and tells him how to go home. The left brain says, "I understand the words, but birds don't speak." The right brain says, "What did the boy say back to the bird?" It understands these impossible developments as facts. In this way story-telling helps the brain to integrate its two sides into a whole, which promotes health and self-realization.

As people listen to stories, they form images in their minds that are stored in the memory as symbols. Studies have shown that humans retain only 20% of what they read, but they recall 80% of symbols, which helps to explain why stories can have such a powerful impact on us.

As for those of you who are apprehensive about telling stories, it is a skill that improves with practice. The most difficult part is starting. How did you learn to swim? - Probably only after nearly drowning at first. How did you learn to ride a bike? - By repeatedly falling off it no doubt. To tell a story well, you need to practise, and the more you practise, the better you get. For those of you who are afraid that you might not remember every word of the story exactly right, the truth is it makes no difference. For no two people ever tell any story the same way. A story is like a letter that comes to us from yesterday. Whoever tells it adds his or her words to the message and then sends it on tomorrow. Moreover, to listen to stories without ever telling one is like harvesting grain without sowing seeds; it is like picking fruit without pruning the trees.

It might also be helpful to bear in mind that we all tell stories, all the time. When someone asks you how your day went, that's an invitation for a story. We then allow the listener to participate in our lives by sharing the interesting highlights of the events we experience. Storytelling in the classroom is merely an extension of what we already do on a daily basis.

Storytelling traditionally begins with a "Once upon a time..." opening and then a storyteller's silent pause to gather his / her thoughts. The traditional openings, of which there are many, were "rituals" that served as a signal that the teller was suspending "time and space" as we know it and trans-porting the audience to a world of imagination and play. They identified the teller and established the audience's commitment to accept for the moment that imaginary world and its "rules". Similar "rituals" also signal the end of the story and their return to reality. However, many adults today have forgotten these "rules of the game."

Intertextuality in literature refers to the way in which a text may invoke other texts and is based on Bakhtin's idea that every utterance has some kind of dialogic relationship with other utterances which have preceded it. The opening "once upon a time" provides an example of this as it brings to mind other fairy tales that are part of our pool of knowledge and gives us an indication of what type of story to expect.

A common feature of religious rhetoric is known as the call and response – when the congregation echoes the words of the preacher or even add words of their own. This device can be made use of to actively engage listeners in the storytelling process and is a common feature of Jamaican storytelling, where the storyteller calls "Anansi" (a character that frequently appears in Jamaican tales) and the listeners respond "Story". In certain Gypsy communities another storytelling convention is made use of. To ensure an attentive audience while telling a story, the storyteller interrupts the narrative to interpolate the word "shoes"; and unless the learners immediately respond "socks", breaks off the tale without finishing it! Storytelling can be regarded as an activity shared by storyteller and story listeners. It is the interaction of the two that makes a story come to life so it is a good idea to create as many opportunities as possible for this to take place.

By choosing to tell rather than read the story, there are a number of advantages to be had. Speakers who rely on scripts are much more restricted when it comes to using non-verbal signals. This is because gestures look very unnatural when not co-oriented with talk that is spontaneous or "off the cuff". If you can tell a story rather than read it, this leaves your hands free to gesture, allows you to make eye contact with your audience and to calibrate for their responses.

Can a story with no identifiable author written or told in vernacular language, be considered to be literary? It would seem to go against the generally accepted idea that literary language represents the best or most prestigious forms of English, and is distinctly different from everyday usage. What counts as art is influenced by conceptions of "literature", which often means printed fiction (poetry, plays and novels), even though in practice language often combines with other media to produce artistic effects. Particular cultures place value on different kinds of English language art. Oral literature has unfortunately lost much of its currency in the dominant literate society of England. But in other cultures, such as in the Caribbean, there are highly regarded forms of storytelling with stylistic features deriving from their oral delivery.

Can a case be made for including folktales in a canon? A canon is the identification of a body of indispensable and authoritative writings. Such texts have always been important for definitions of what counts as Standard English. Samuel Johnson, for example, based his dictionary on books which he believed illustrated authoritative uses and meanings of the language. The traditional canon relies exclusively on the printed word and assumes a distance between writer and reader. Most folktales do not fit this description. However, literature in a canon, which is a pool of shared knowledge, can have a bonding purpose. People can respond to references to it, as to other shared cultural texts such as fairy tales and this definition could justify the inclusion of folktales in such a collection.

Whether folktales can be considered to be literary or not is clearly debatable. However, we can say without any doubt at all that stories offer us doorways into new ways of seeing and being in the world, and surely there can be no greater justification for using them than that.

The Lay-out and the Contents

This workbook consists of a collection of 60 traditional and contemporary tales, graded Pre-intermediate, Intermediate, Upper Intermediate or Advanced, with accompanying worksheets. The notes for teachers that go with each tale include *pre-listening*, *while-listening*, and *post-listening* tasks, as well as a key with the answers to all the exercises.

Stories not only entertain; they can also alter our experience so as to facilitate growth and change, and the tales included in this book have all been chosen with this aim in mind. Storytellers, unlike folklorists, who make statistical samplings of all the stories they have gathered, choose in the end those stories they believe in, which is what I have done for this collection. However, at the same time, in selecting which tales to include, their length was a factor and also their subject matter. Stories have been chosen that deal with the topics that tend to be featured in course books so they can be incorporated into an integrated programme.

Ways of Promoting Storytelling in the Classroom

Telling stories is one of the basic ways that humans communicate with each other. When you tell your partner about your day at the office, you are telling a story. When you repeat a joke you have heard, you are in effect telling a story. It is something we do all the time without even realizing that we are doing so. Here are five ways of promoting storytelling in the classroom that require hardly any preparation and that enable you to sit back, relax (more or less) and let the learners do all the work:

True Stories

We can draw on a variety of sources to construct stories - personal tales or stories of real experiences that friends, colleagues, or members of our families have had. Here are some questions to stir memories. Ask the learners each to pick one and then to pair up and tell each other the stories that the prompts help them to recall:

- Have you ever been badly hurt?
- Have you ever been really scared?
- Did you ever play a practical joke on someone? Have you ever had one played on you?
- Have you ever done something you are proud of, something heroic, or something brave?
- Have you ever been in a really dangerous situation?
- What happened to you when you were a child that you would like to share?

Feelings

First of all, to start the process off, ask each member of the class to pick a number between one and fifty, but to keep that number a secret. In other words, not to tell anyone else what it is at this stage.

Then ask them to go to their number on a list (that can be provided on a hand-out or shown on an OHP) where they will find an adjective next to the number they chose. Ask them to think about the last time something happened to make them feel this way, and then to tell the person sitting next to them about the occasion:

1. proud 2. alienated 3. hopeful 4. terrified 5. envious 6. impressed 7. desperate 8. competitive 9. blessed 10. ashamed 11. incompetent 12. rejected 13. disappointed 14. confident 15. peaceful 16. honoured 17. humiliated 18. disgusted 19. rebellious 20. embarrassed 21. hateful 22. grateful 23. shy 24. masterful 25. loving 26. confused 27. resentful 28. shocked 29. angry 30. brave 31. adventurous 32. privileged 33. sorry 34. annoyed 35. ignored 36. misunderstood 37. amazed 38. relieved 39. accepted 40. sad 41. cowardly 42. defeated 43. loyal 44. victorious 45. enlightened 46. obsessed 47. foolish 48. lonely 49. guilty 50. joyful

Then invite anyone who heard an interesting story to tell the whole class about it.

An alternative approach would be to invite the learners to reflect on what emotions they have experienced over the last 24 hours – maybe happiness, anxiety, surprise, anger, fear, or something else - then to choose one, and tell the person sitting next to them about it.

Origins

Everything has a story because everything comes, in its elemental form, from the Earth. Invite the learners to choose an item from the following list of "things" and to imagine its life story. Then ask them to describe the history of the item backwards through the personal use, purchase, manufacture, to original natural resources from which it or its components were made. They can personify the thing and tell its story like an autobiography.

- a newspaper
- a leather handbag
- a diamond ring
- a wig (made of real hair)
- a pair of woollen socks
- a cigar
- a necklace of pearls
- a fur coat

The activity "Dead Man on the Circle Line" offers another way of exploring origins. A passenger dies on the Circle Line and spends several hours going round and round before a fellow passenger notices and informs a member of staff. The corpse is taken to hospital but no documents are found on the body to identify the person. The only clues they have are the contents of the briefcase the passenger had with him.

Invite the learners to each make a list of the contents of the briefcase (5 items only) on a piece of paper. Collect in the slips of paper and re-distribute them, making sure nobody gets their own list back. Then ask the recipients of the lists to use the information they have to build up a picture of the poor unfortunate person whose body was found.

Story Recipes

Arrange the learners in circles of eight. Ask them to look through the sections below and choose one element from each of them (allow each member of the circle to make one of the choices). Then invite each group to write a collective story that incorporates all the elements chosen. (Alternatively, to make the activity more improvisational in nature, put each element on a card and invite the members of each circle to randomly select one item from each category).

Characters (you can choose two):

- boy
- girl
- animal
- man
- woman
- idea
- spirit
- machine
- thing
- plant

Location:

- farm
- village
- otherworldly
- city
- mountains
- forest
- ocean
- desert

Time:

- A long time ago
- Now
- In the future

Problem:

- Caught stealing
- Told a lie
- Saw or heard a secret
- Lost something
- Been captured
- Under a spell or curse
- Goes to a forbidden place
- Finds a forbidden object
- Has an enemy
- Causes jealousy
- Forgets something
- Broke something
- Does not like something
- Needs to escape or hide
- Needs to rescue someone or something
- Needs to prove worth

Inner Trait that causes the Original Problem:

- Is greedy
- Doesn't follow advice
- Is lazy
- Is pessimistic
- Is blindly in love
- Is angry & seeks revenge
- Is naive & trusting
- Is clumsy
- Lacks confidence
- Is foolish

Inner Trait that lead to a Solution:

- Is courageous
- Is resourceful
- Is kind
- Is generous
- Is clever
- Is loyal
- Is strong
- Is optimistic

Solution:

- Has a magical helper
- Has a non-magical helper
- Is rescued
- Is transformed
- Discovers a skill
- Exercises cleverness
- Uses inner traits
- Undertakes a journey

Conclusion:

- Is rewarded
- Is wiser
- Is transformed
- Comes with a gift or treasure
- Lives well
- Passes luck or a reward on to others
- Has a positive impact on the world
- Offers wisdom

Stories from Proverbs

Have students choose a proverb from the list below. Then ask them to work in groups and to develop a story, for which the proverb serve as moral:

- One finger cannot lift a pebble. (Iranian)
- When elephants battle, the ants perish. (Cambodian)
- If you chase two hares, you will not catch either. (Russian)
- It is better to turn back than to get lost. (Russian)
- Handsome words don't butter cabbage. (German)
- Talk does not cook rice. (Chinese)
- After the rain, there is no need for an umbrella. (Bulgaria)
- When the kettle boils over, it overflows its own sides. (Yiddish)
- You can't chew with somebody else's teeth. (Yiddish)
- Mistrust is an axe at the tree of love. (Russian)
- If a farmer becomes a King, he will still carry a basket on his back. (Hebrew)
- Not all that is black is charcoal. (Philippine)
- Little brooks make great rivers. (French)
- Every kind of animal can be tamed, but not the tongue of man. (Philippine)
- Do not look for apples under a poplar tree. (Slovakian)

- Every ass loves to hear himself bray. (English)
- He that goes barefoot must not plant thorns. (English)
- Better to be a free bird than a captive King. (Danish)
- A blow passes on, a spoken word lingers. (Yiddish)
- You can't spit on my back and make me think it's rain. (Yiddish)
- A book gives knowledge, but it is life that gives understanding. (Hebrew)
- A crooked branch has a crooked shadow. (Japanese)
- Better bread with water than cake with trouble. (Russian)
- The heaviest burden is an empty pocket. (Yiddish)
- A candle lights others but consumes itself. (English)
- It takes a village to raise a child. (Africa)
- It is one thing to cackle and another to lay an egg. (Ecuador)
- One dog barks because it sees something; a hundred dogs bark because they heard the first dog bark. (Chinese)
- To hide one lie, a thousand lies are needed. (India)
- A needle wrapped in a rag will be found in the end. (Vietnamese)
- Do not seek to escape from the flood by clinging to a tiger's tail. (Chinese)
- Step by step one ascends the staircase. (Turkey)
- Anger is a bad adviser. (Hungary)
- Eggs must not quarrel with stones. (Jamaican)
- Eyes can see everything except themselves. (Serbo-Croatian)
- Haste makes waste. (English)
- Every hill has its valley. (Italian)

CARRYING AND LEAVING

Level: Pre-Intermediate / Intermediate
Target Audience: Adults
Language / Skills Focus: Listening & Speaking
Materials: Photocopies of the worksheet to hand out after the storytelling

IN CLASS

1. *Pre-listening:* What do you do with your troubles at the end of the day? Do you continue to carry them around with you or are you able to put them to one side, to forget about them? That's what the story you're going to hear is all about.

2. *While-listening:* Pause after "Oh, so that's been bothering you! Brother ..." and ask the learners to predict the ending.

3. *Post-listening:* What do you do to turn off and relax at the end of the day? Invite the learners to discuss this question in pairs or small groups, then to report back with their findings.

4. Place the parts of the story in the correct order: 1-e 2-a 3-f 4-i 5-h 6-c 7-d 8-g 9-b

5. Match the numbers on the left with the letters on the right to find explanations for the new vocabulary: 1-h 2-e 3-f 4-a 5-d 6-g 7-j 8-i 9-b 10-c 11-k

COMMENTS

This story, a Buddhist parable, is a helpful metaphor for looking at how to manage stress. It allows us to call into question the "vows" by which we judge ourselves and, as a result, to be more forgiving. Then hopefully, like the monk, having done his best in the situation, we can let go of the past and move on.

THE STORY

Once upon a time, there were two monks who went on a pilgrimage across the country together. After some time, they came to a riverbank and saw a beautiful girl who was unable to cross the river.

Seeing her difficulty, the elder monk volunteered to carry her across the river on his back while the younger one looked on in consternation.

When the sun went down, the monks came upon a dilapidated shack and decided to stay there for the night. The elder monk quickly fell asleep while the younger one twisted around, unable to calm his mind. Finally, he woke up the elder monk and reprimanded him for what had happened during the day, "As monks, we're supposed to keep away from women. I'm really ashamed and troubled by what you did today!"

The elder monk looked at his friend and a smile appeared on his face, "Oh, so that's been bothering you! Brother, I've left the girl behind by the river bank, why are you still carrying her around?"

CARRYNG AND LEAVNG: WORKSHEET

Place the nine parts of the story in the correct order:

   a. After some time, they came to a riverbank and saw a beautiful girl who was unable to cross the river.

   b. Brother, I've left the girl behind by the river bank, why are you still carrying her around?"

   c. Finally, he woke up the elder monk and reprimanded him for what had happened during the day, "As monks, we're supposed to keep away from women.

   d. I'm really ashamed and troubled by what you did today!"

   e. Once upon a time, there were two monks who went on a pilgrimage across the country together.

   f. Seeing her difficulty, the elder monk volunteered to carry her across the river on his back while the younger one looked on in consternation.

   g. The elder monk looked at his friend and a smile appeared on his face, "Oh, so that's been bothering you!

   h. The elder monk quickly fell asleep while the younger one twisted around, unable to calm his mind.

   i. When the sun went down, the monks came upon a dilapidated shack and decided to stay there for the night.

ANSWERS: 1 ___ 2 ___ 3 ___ 4 ___ 5 ___ 6 ___ 7 ___ 8 ___ 9 ___

Match the numbers on the left with the letters on the right to find explanations for the new vocabulary:

1. monks	a. anxiously
2. a pilgrimage	b. criticised
3. volunteered	c. embarrassed by
4. in consternation	d. found by chance
5. came upon	e. a journey to a place of religious importance
6. dilapidated	f. offered
7. shack	g. old and in bad condition
8. calm his mind	h. religious men who live apart from other people
9. reprimanded	i. stop worrying
10. ashamed	j. a small, simple building
11. bothering	k. upsetting / disturbing

CARRYING AND LEAVING: WORKSHEET - HOW STRESSED OUT ARE YOU?

1. How do you react when something upsets you or winds you up?

    a. You think about it for a day or two.

    b. You can't get it out of your head for a week or more.

    c. Your thoughts quickly turn to other things.

2. How do you feel when you think about all the jobs you have to do during the day?

    a. You usually feel you can cope well despite the pressures.

    b. You feel wound up but expect to get through it.

    c. You feel overwhelmed and think you'll never be able to do them.

3. How does your body feel on a typical day?

    a. Tense across the neck and shoulders.

    b. Relaxed. Your breathing is always easy and slow.

    c. Very stiff in the neck and shoulders and you're prone to frequent headaches.

4. How do you react to the situations you find yourself in during the course of an average day?

    a. You tend to lose your temper over unimportant things.

    b. You get more irritated by things going wrong then you would like.

    c. You cope calmly with life's usual setbacks.

5. What's your sleeping pattern like?

    a. You have no problems sleeping.

    b. You wake up frequently during the night and often feel tired the next day.

    c. You get odd nights of bad sleep but can usually make up for them.

6. How do you react when you think of what other people expect from you in life?

    a. You panic and feel inadequate.

    b. You can keep a sense of perspective. You know there are lots of things you can't do, and that's fine.

    c . You take their opinions seriously but you don't lose any sleep over them.

CHECK YOUR SCORES:

1   a-2 b-3 c-1

2   a-1 b-2 c-3

3   a-2 b-1 c-3

4   a-3 b-2 c-1

5   a-1 b-3 c-2

6   a-3 b-1 c-2

WHAT YOUR SCORE MEANS:

11 – 18 You clearly feel stressed out and need to do something about it. Make sure you do some regular exercise or take up meditation or yoga. Reduce your intake of stimulants such as nicotine and caffeine. Eat non-fatty, wholesome starchy foods and avoid sugars. Most important of all, learn how to say no.

10 – 14 Your stress levels are about average, but you should do what you can to lower them so read the tips above.

6 – 9 You're doing well and have nothing to worry about. We live in a stressful world but it's obvious you can cope. You can set a good example for those around you to follow so they can learn how to keep their stress levels under control too.

THE MONKEY WHO COULD NOT SLEEP

Level: Intermediate - Advanced
Target Audience: Secondary
Language / Skills Focus: Listening, Speaking & Writing / Topic-based Idioms
Materials: Photocopies of the worksheet. Photocopies of the story (optional) to hand out at the end of the session.

IN CLASS

1   *Pre-listening*: Hand out the worksheets and start with the pair-work interviews. The learners can then report back to the class with their findings. While this is taking place, make a note of the effective language used and any errors that crop up, which you can then deal with at the end of the session.

2   *Post-listening*: Ask the class what they think the monkey dreamt of when he finally fell asleep. Then arrange the students in small groups to work on a story entitled "The Monkey's Dream".

3   The cloze test and the Animal Idioms exercise on the worksheet are intended for higher level classes and can be set for homework.

CLOZE TEST: 1. why 2. remains 3. although 4. about 5. for 6. in 7. part 8. as 9. amount 10. by 11. there 12. which 13. for 14. more 15. as 16. for 17. appears 18. necessary 19. remain 20. with

ANIMAL IDIOMS: a. cat b. dog c. pig d. horse e. fish f. duck g. monkey h. bird i. rat j. donkey k. bees l. parrot

THE STORY

Once upon a time there was a monkey who lived in a tree. The forest had always been quiet and the monkey could sleep undisturbed whenever it wanted to. But one night the frogs made so much noise that the monkey could not sleep a wink.

The next morning he paid them a visit. "Why did you make so much noise last night?" he asked. "I couldn't sleep at all!"

"We are sorry," said the frogs, "but we were laughing at the turtle because he spent the whole night carrying his house from one place to the other. He still has it on his back now and he doesn't know where to put it. He looks so funny!"

So the monkey went to visit the turtle. "Why do you carry your house on your back like that?" he asked.

"Oh, it's the firefly! I'm afraid that he'll burn down my house because he always flies around

14

with a torch," answered the turtle.

Monkey visited the firefly next. The firefly said, "I'm afraid of the mosquito. I carry a fire so I'll know when he's near in case he tries to sting me!"

The monkey asked the mosquito to do something about his stinging so that the other animals would not make so much noise. The mosquito promised, "All right, before I sting anyone I'll make a buzzing sound to warn them I'm near. The firefly won't need a fire to know that I'm around if I do that."

Relieved, the monkey went to his tree. "At last, I can sleep!" he exclaimed.

THE MONKEY WHO COULD NOT SLEEP: WORKSHEET

Work in pairs. Take it in turns to ask each other the following questions, then report back to the class with your findings:

a. How many hours do you sleep on average a night?
b. Do you ever have trouble in getting to sleep and what do you do when you find yourself in this situation?
c. Have you ever fallen asleep in class, at work or travelling on public transport? Tell me about it.
d. Do you talk or walk in your sleep or do you know anyone who does? Tell me about it.
e. How often do you dream and do you remember what you dream about?
f. Have you ever had a premonition in a dream that came true? Tell me about it.
g. What would you do if your neighbours were having a party and making so much noise that you couldn't get to sleep?
h. What do you know about the interpretation of dreams or dream analysis?

What do you think the monkey dreamt of when he finally fell asleep? Working in small groups, work on a story entitled "The Monkey's Dream"

Fill each of the numbered gaps in the following passage with one suitable word: Exactly 1. ..... we sleep and dream still 2. ..... a mystery. 3. ..... much has been discovered 4. .... our need 5. ..... sleep there is still much to learn. 6. ..... good health sleep is a normal 7. ..... of living just 8. ..... any other natural function is. The 9. ..... of sleep required 10. ..... an individual varies. 11. ..... is no "right" amount of sleep 12. ..... is adequate 13. ..... all. Generally we need 14. ..... sleep when we are younger, and less 15. ..... we age. 16. ..... an adult, six to eight hours 17. ..... to be the average amount of sleep 18. ..... for good health. However, many people 19. ..... alert and well 20. ..... only a few hours of sleep daily.

ANIMAL IDIOMS: Use the following words to complete the sentences:

bees / bird / cat / dog / donkey / duck / fish / horse / monkey / parrot / pig / rat

a. I'm sorry to disappoint you but you haven't got a.....in hell's chance.

b. You've been leading me a.....'s life and I've had as much as I can take.

c. Don't be so greedy. Stop making a.....of yourself!

d. You're flogging a dead.....by asking him to lend you the money. It's like trying to get blood out of a stone!

e. As I didn't know anybody there, I felt like a.....out of water.

f. However much you criticise her, it has no effect at all. It's like water off a.....'s back.

g. I wasn't born yesterday, you know. You can't make a.....out of me!

h. How did you find out that I was getting married?
  - A little.....told me!

i. There's something funny going on around here. I think I smell a.....!

j. Why do I always have to do the.....work? Why don't you offer to do it for a change?

k. My parents never told me about the birds and the..... I suppose they found it too embar-rassing.

l. Don't learn these idioms.....fashion. Make sure you understand and know how to use them!

WHY KANGAROOS HAVE A POUCH

Level: Intermediate – Advanced
Target Audience: Secondary / Adults
Language / Skills Focus: Listening & Speaking
Materials: Photocopies of the worksheet. Photocopies of the story (optional) to hand out at the end of the session. A kangaroo mask / costume (optional) if you can find or make one.

IN CLASS

1   As a lead-in to the story you can start with a brainstorming session: *What can you tell me about kangaroos?* Then go into the following routine:

"We're very fortunate to have the opportunity today to interview a talking kangaroo! Work in small groups and make a list of questions you'd like to ask our celebrity:" (Give some sample questions to start the process off).

TEACHER TO STUDENT: *Have you got any kangaroos in Kiev?*
STUDENT TO TEACHER: *No!*
TEACHER TO STUDENT: *Well, you've got one now because you've just become one! I'd like you to come up to the front and to sit on this chair to answer everyone's questions.*

2   For a post-listening activity, you can arrange the students in groups to make up parallel stories while you circulate to provide any assistance required. A spokesperson for each group can then tell their story to the rest of the class and they can be produced in written form for homework. Here are some possible titles: *Why Elephants Have Tusks / Why Camels Have Humps / Why Dalmations Have Spots / Why Loch Ness Has A Monster / Why Bees Have Stings /Why Snails Carry Their Homes On Their Backs*

3   The worksheet consists of a matching activity to help with some of the vocabulary presented in the story, and a cloze test for high level students that can lead into work on the issue of animal rights. Here are the suggested answers:

Read through the story to find words in which mean the same as the following: a. wobbled weakly towards her / b. I'm old and I'm useless, no good to myself or anyone else. / c. Come on now, cheer up / d. Then fear gave way to determination to save the old fellow. / e. alerted by the noise / f. she hopped full speed into the bush / g. she would be killed if she could not keep out of reach / **h.** walking dejectedly back to camp / i. had finally given up the chase / j. pretended to be helpless / k. was so touched by her concern for all his creatures

ANIMAL RIGHTS: 1. by 2. of 3. towards 4. for 5. to 6. on 7. against 8. in 9. for 10. on 11. After 12. For 13. to 14. on 15. for 16. against 17. on 18. on 19. to 20. to

WHY KANGAROOS HAVE A POUCH: WORKSHEET

Read through the story to find words which mean the same as the following:

a. approached her looking as if he was on his last legs

b. I'm nothing more than a waste of space.

c. That's no way to talk - don't be so miserable.

d. Although she was frightened, this made her want to try even harder to help her friend

e. made aware of the danger by her attempts to distract the hunter

f. moved as quickly as she could into an area where she wouldn't be spotted

g. would lose her life if she were caught

h. returned to camp looking completely fed up

i. had at long last realized he was wasting his time

j. made it seem as if he was weaker then he really was

k. was so moved by the consideration she showed towards others

ANIMAL RIGHTS Supply the missing prepositions:

As members of human society we live 1. _____ moral codes designed to protect our weaker members. We take care 2. _____ the sick, old and disabled and punish those who are violent 3. _____ others. These qualities of compassion and justice are part of being human. But we also have a darker side which is responsible 4. _____ violence and destruction. It is 5. _____ these aspects of human nature which vivisection appeals. We experiment 6. _____ animals because they are powerless to stop us and we count their pain as unimportant when measured 7. _____ our own interests. We live unhealthy lives and make animals suffer 8. _____ the search for cures 9. _____ our ills. We even see the production of a new lipstick or oven cleaner as a good enough reason to inflict pain 10. _____ animals. It's not that we think animals can't feel pain - we know very well that they do. And it is dangerous to say that we use animals in experiments because they lack our intelligence. 11. _____ all, this argument would also allow us to experiment on mentally handicapped humans. We use animals because we have decided that our species is so important that other species should suffer 12. _____ our benefit. Animals have feelings. Like us, they can suffer pain, fear and mental agony. Like us, each has a life to live. A rat's life is important 13. _____ a rat whatever value a human may place 14. _____ it! Why should one individual animal be made to suffer 15. _____ the supposed benefit of people (or other animals)? Would it be right to kill one human being in an experiment if it would save thousands of others? What if the human were you?

As important as it is, the case 16. _____ vivisection does not rely 17. _____ the mass of evidence which shows that it is bad science. It rests 18. _____ the belief that it is morally wrong to deliberately harm those weaker than ourselves - whether they belong 19. _____ our own, or 20. _____ another species.

WHY KANGAROOS HAVE A POUCH

The Kangaroo mother was very worried. Her young joey was always getting lost and she had to watch him all the time. One day while she was in the bush, carefully watching her joey as usual, an old wombat wobbled weakly towards her.

'Ohhh! Ohhh! I'm old and I'm useless, no good to myself or anyone else,' she heard him mumbling as he came near. Poor thing, she thought, he looks really miserable.

'Come on now, cheer up,' she said brightly; but even in the oldest time no-one cheered up just because they were told to.

'Cheer up?' said the wombat. 'How can I, when I'm blind and can't find fresh grass to eat. Nobody cares about me, no-one bothers to be kind or helpful, and I haven't got a friend in the whole wide world.'

The kangaroo felt really sorry for him. 'I'll be your friend,' she said. 'I'll lead you to some fresh grass and some cool water, too.'

She showed him how to take hold of her tail, and in this way was able to lead him, very carefully, to the water. He drank deeply of the cold running water, and then held her tail again as she hopped off slowly towards a patch of fresh grass she had seen nearby. He was so weak that he lost hold of her tail several times, confused by his blindness, but each time she patiently stopped and helped him.

When they arrived at the good patch of grass, the old wombat sniffed at the fresh grass and began to munch it. The kangaroo felt really pleased as she saw how happy he was. But suddenly she remembered her joey, and quickly bounded back to where she had left him. Of course, he had hopped away and become lost again.

Anxiously she started searching for him, and this time was lucky. After only a few minutes she found him - fast asleep in the shade of a gum-tree.

'He looks quite comfortable and safe,' she thought. 'I won't disturb him.' And she left him there while she hurried back to see if the blind wombat was still enjoying his feast. Suddenly she stopped, her heart thumping wildly. An aboriginal hunter was stalking the defenceless wombat.

The hunter was holding his spear high, ready to attack. Closer and closer he crept. The kangaroo watched in horror for a moment. Then fear gave way to determination to save the old fellow. She started jumping about wildly, crackling fallen twigs and thumping the ground until she had attracted the hunter's attention. If he chased after her, the wombat - alerted by the noise – would have time to hide.

Just as she planned, as soon as the hunter's sharp eyes saw a kangaroo, he forgot the wombat. Off she hopped full speed into the bush, her heart beating wildly for she knew she would be killed if she could not keep out of reach. She dodged in and out among the trees and bushes, but the hunter was quick and agile, and followed closely.

After a long chase she came upon a secluded cave, Trembling with fear and exhaustion she hurried inside, and the hunter ran past without noticing the cave. For a while she stayed there, too afraid to move; but at last she saw the hunter walking dejectedly back to camp. He had finally given up the chase.

As soon as he was out of sight the kangaroo hurried back, frightened for her baby. Quite safe, he had just woken up and was very pleased to see her. Together they hopped - very slowly because the joey was only small - back to the good patch of grass. The kangaroo wanted to see the wombat to make sure he was all right and tell him about the hunter; so she was disappointed to find that the old fellow had gone.

'I hope he'll be all right,' she said to her joey. 'I did feel so sorry for him.'

What she didn't know was that the old blind wombat wasn't a wombat at all. Byamee, the great father-of-all, had come down from the sky world and pretended to be helpless so that he could discover which was the kindest of all his creatures. And back in the sky world he was smiling. He was smiling because he had certainly found the kindest animal of all.

He decided to reward the kangaroo, and he knew exactly what gift she would most appreciate.

He called one of his spirit friends and told him, 'Go down to the earth world. Go make a dilly bag apron from the string of bark, and when you have finished it, give it to the kangaroo mother. Tell her the whole story, and explain that she must tie the dilly bag around her waist.'

When the spirit friend had done all this, and the kangaroo tied on the dilly bag, Byamee magically made it grow to her body. How happy she was when she realised she had a pouch to put her joey in so that he would be safe. He could sleep snugly in it, or peep out at the world as his mother hopped along.

However, Byamee was right. This kangaroo was the kindest of all. She worried that the other kangaroo mothers were not as lucky as she was. She worried too about her cousins, the wallabies, the little kangaroo rats and all the rest.

Byamee, the great god in the sky world, was so touched by her concern for all his creatures that he sent a message saying he had decided to make pouches grow on the bodies of all the gentle mothers of the marsupial family. And there was great joy in the kangaroo world. How good it felt to be cared for so kindly!

I KNOW BUT …

Level: Intermediate – Advanced
Target Audience: Secondary, Adults
Language / Skills Focus: Listening & Speaking
Materials: Photocopies of the worksheets. Photocopies of the story (optional) to hand out at the end of the session.

IN CLASS

1   *Pre-listening*: Ask the learners to listen to the story, and then decide which of the suggested morals below is the most appropriate. Alternatively, if none of the options appeal, you can ask the students to find a moral of their own. at the moral is. And if they don't like the suggestions, they can find a moral of their own!

    a. Make hay while the sun shines.
    b. Strike while the iron is hot.
    c. A stitch in time saves nine.
    d. Don't put off until tomorrow what you can do today.
    e. It's easy to be wise after the event.
    f. It's no use crying over spilt milk.
    g. You can lead a horse to water but you can't make him drink.

2   Some people seem to devote most of their energy to making excuses for not acting. Invite the learners to think of something they currently feel they need to do in their lives and then ask them what excuses they make use of to avoid acting. The consequences of such behaviour can be disastrous and that's what the tale that follows is all about.

3   *While-listening*: Ask the learners to stop you / the CD player as soon as they have worked out what kind of creatures George and Harriet are.

4   *Post-listening*: Hand out the worksheets for the learners to work on individually or in pairs. The answers are presented below:

The Matching Activity: 1-f 2-l 3-n 4-a 5-m 6-g 7-b 8-k 9-h 10-i 11-j 12-d 13-c 14-e

True or False? 1-True 2-False 3-True 4-False 5-True 6-True 7-False 8-False

Multiple Choice: 1-d / 2-d / 3-b / 4-b / 5-b / 6-d

5   While the role play is taking place, circulate to make a note of the effective language being

used as well as any errors that crop up. These can then be dealt with at the end of the session.

A: You need to learn a language in order to get a new job / promotion but you can't be bothered and keep putting it off. Your partner's going to try once again to persuade you to act but you just want a quiet life and are perfectly happy the way you are.

B: Your partner needs to learn a new language in order to get a new job / promotion but he / she can't be bothered and keeps finding excuses for not acting. You're fed up with this and determined to bring about change.

6   To conclude the session, you might like to put the following questions to the class as a whole:
a. Did any change take place in your partner as a result of your conversation? Why / why not?
b. What have you learnt from today's story? And what changes, if any, will you make to your life as a result?

I KNOW BUT …

"Only five more collecting days to go before winter hibernation," Harriet said. She nudged George with her elbow in an attempt to rouse him from his sleep.

"I know but it's so warm and cosy here in this tree trunk that I think I'll just take it easy today," he replied.

Then he rolled over and drifted off again. In fact, he slept right through until the following morning.

"Just four days left now," Harriet reminded George the next day when he woke up.

"I know but we've still got food left. I wish you wouldn't worry so much. I promise I'll go collecting tomorrow."

George covered himself with his blanket of twigs and leaves and returned to his nut-filled dreams once more. And another day was lost.

"There's only three days to go now and you haven't even started collecting." Harriet was beginning to get anxious. "Remember the little ones. We've got three new mouths to feed now."

"I know but the owner of the house is sure to leave us a pile of nuts on the garden wall - he always does."

George made himself comfortable and went back to sleep again. Harriet spent the day trying to keep herself busy and so another day passed.

"Two days left. The owner of the house has left us nothing this year. I went outside earlier on to check. I think he's gone away on holiday. I peeped through the bedroom window yesterday and I saw him packing his suitcase. He's probably gone to spend Christmas with his mother this year. You've got to do something George." Harriet was getting desperate.

"I know but it's freezing cold outside and raining so I'll wait until tomorrow when the weather clears up. Come snuggle up beside me and that way we'll both be able to keep warm. George slept but Harriet couldn't because she knew of the danger they faced. And so another day came and went.

"George you've really got to do something today. It's your very last chance." Harriet tried once again to stir her man into action.

"I know but we've still got a few nuts left from last year. And with a bit of luck they should last us. After all, once we're asleep we won't need anything. Trust me. I know what I'm doing."

"I know but ..." Harriet started but never finished her sentence. She realised she was beginning to sound just like George.

And so the winter hibernation began with George and Harriet's storehouse empty despite the fact that they had three new mouths to feed.

When spring came round once more, George and Harriet woke from their winter sleep but the three babies didn't. The poor little souls had starved to death.

 "This is all your fault George," said Harriet. "I kept telling you to prepare for the winter but you did nothing. If you'd spent all the energy you put into inventing excuses on gathering nuts, our babies would still be alive."
"I know but not to worry. Life will be easier with three fewer mouths to feed and we can always try again for babies. In fact, we could start right now."

But Harriet wasn't interested. And from that day on they both slept in separate beds. George and Harriet never did have any more children and George kept saying "I know but ..." until his dying day.

I KNOW BUT: WORKSHEET 1

Listen to the story, and then decide what the moral is:

a. Make hay while the sun shines.

b. Strike while the iron is hot.

c. A stitch in time saves nine.

d. Don't put off until tomorrow what you can do today.

e. It's easy to be wise after the event.

f. It's no use crying over spilt milk.

g. You can lead a horse to water but you can't make him drink.

Match the numbers on the left with the letters on the right to find explanations for the new vocabulary:

1.	nudged	a.	comfortable and warm
2.	elbow	b.	covering of small branches
3.	rouse him	c.	died from lack of food
4.	cosy	d.	encourage her man to do something constructive
5.	trunk	e.	finding reasons for not acting
6.	reminded George	f.	gently pushed
7.	blanket of twigs	g.	made George remember
8.	beginning to get anxious	h.	looked secretly
9.	peeped	i.	losing hope
10.	getting desperate	j.	move into a warm and comfortable position
11.	snuggle up	k.	starting to get worried
12.	stir her man into action	l.	the joint in the middle of the arm
13.	starved to death	m.	the main part of a tree
14.	inventing excuses	n.	wake him up

Decide whether the following statements are *True* or *False*:

1. George and Harriet were two squirrels who lived in a tree.

2. They were a childless couple.

3. George was an expert at finding excuses for doing nothing.

4. The owner of the house left them a pile of nuts on the wall before going on holiday.

5. George and Harriet slept all through the winter.

6. When they woke up they found that their children were dead.

7. Harriet wanted to try again for babies.

8. They never had any more children and George never said 'I know but ...' again.

I KNOW BUT: WORKSHEET 2

Complete each of the statements by choosing the answer you think fits best:

1. Harriet and George were
   a. both birds who lived in a nest.
   b. both rabbits who lived in a hole in the ground.
   c. both frogs and they lived in the garden pond.
   d. both squirrels and lived inside a tree.

2. Harriet wanted George to collect food
   a. for their holiday.
   b. for Christmas.
   c. to feed their babies.
   d. to prepare for the winter.

3. The owner of the house
   a. always left them food on the garden wall.
   b. was friendly towards them.
   c. was hostile towards them.
   d. lived with his mother.

4. George didn't want to collect food because
   a. the weather was cold.
   b. he was lazy.
   c. he wasn't hungry.
   d. he didn't want to feed the babies.

5. The three babies died
   a. from the cold.
   b. from lack of food.
   c. because they were ill.
   d. because nobody cared about them.

6. After the babies died,
   a. George changed his ways.
   b. George stopped loving Harriet.
   c. George blamed himself for what had happened.
   d. Harriet never fully forgave George.

A ROLE PLAY

A: You need to learn a new language in order to get a job / promotion but you can't be bothered and keep putting it off. Your partner's going to try once again to persuade you to act but you just want a quiet life and are perfectly happy the way you are.

B: Your partner needs to learn a new language in order to get a job / promotion but he / she can't be bothered and keeps finding excuses for not acting. You're fed up with this and determined to bring about change.

MADAME QIN

Level: Upper Intermediate - Advanced
Target Audience: Adults
Language / Skills Focus: Listening, Speaking & Writing
Materials: Photocopies of the worksheets. Photocopies of the story (optional) to hand out at the end of the session.

IN CLASS

1. *Pre-Listening:* Pair-work Interviews to provide a lead-in to the topic. Arrange the learners in pairs and invite them to take it in turns to ask each other the questions. They then report back to the rest of the class with their findings. With larger classes, you can arrange the students into two circles for the feedback stage to speed up the process.

2. *Post-Listening:* A word-building game. By answering the clues across, the word "super-natural" is formed in one of the vertical columns. The clues are all idioms related to the topic with missing words to be found. The learners can work on the acrostic in pairs, and then combine into groups of four to compare their answers. The group who finish the activity first can be invited to the front to board their answers and so give the slower groups a helping hand. ANSWERS: 1. between 2. ghost 3. angels 4. loose 5. fury 6. pay 7. hell 8. fairy 9. hunt 10. earth 11. water 12. Soul 13. spirit 14. road 15. spell

3. "How Well Are You Ageing?" After pre-teaching new vocabulary, arrange the students in groups. Hand out a copy of the questionnaire to an "interviewer" in each group who reads the questions to the other students and takes on the role of the teacher. Only the interviewer should be able to see the copy and he/she presents the questionnaire to the group as a listening activity. Meanwhile, you can circulate to provide any assistance required. The next stage is for the learners to add up their scores and assess the results, which can be examined and discussed by the class as a whole. Although the material is inauthentic in that the questionnaire is contrived, the students have an authentic reason for doing the activity - to find out more about themselves.

WHAT YOUR SCORE MEANS

75-100   You tend to turn any careless remark about age into a personal attack. Try not to be so sensitive. On the credit side, you have a lively mind and you're interested in new developments. If you can learn how to live each day to the full and to stop watching the clock, you'll stay young at heart forever.

50-74   You make a good attempt to overcome the fear of growing old but it's there in the background, waiting to pounce, the moment your guard is down. Learn to change what you can and to accept what you can't.

25-49   You admit that old age frightens you and you're determined to fight against it. However, you need to relax a bit. Don't get old before your time - age may not be as close as you think.

0 -24   You're well-balanced and accept the natural pattern of life so you don't see any reason to worry. You move with the time at a gentle pace and will be well prepared for old age when it does come.

COMMENTS

The story, a traditional tale from China, is about an old woman who has a near-death experience, from which she returns with information about the after-life. It was taken from *Chinese Folk Tales* by Howard Giskin, NTC Publishing Group 1997. For a detailed analysis of the story, please see "Soul Loss and the Shamanic Story" by Michael Berman, Cambridge Scholars Publishing, 2008.

MADAME QIN: WORKSHEET 1

Work in pairs and ask each other the following questions. Then report back to the group with your findings:

a. Do you believe in life after death and what form do you think it takes?

b. If you could have the choice, would you like to live forever?

c. If you only had six months left to live, how would you choose to spend your time?

d. Would you like to be buried or cremated? Give reasons for the choice you make.

e. How do you feel about the possibility of your body being frozen, to be resuscitated at some point in the future when a cure to the cause of your death has been found?

f. If you could be born again, would you choose to come back as a baby boy or a girl? And what kind of parents would you choose to be born to?

g. Which charity would you like to leave money to in your will, and why?

Answer the clues across to complete the grid:

1. I feel I'm.....the devil and the deep blue sea and
    I don't know what to do for the best.
2. You haven't got the.....of a chance.
3. Fools rush in where.....fear to tread.
4. As soon as the teacher left the classroom, all
    hell broke.....

5. Hell hath no.....like a woman scorned.
6. Unless you apologise for all the trouble
    you've caused, there's going to be hell to.....
7. I've never seen such a terrifying sight before - it
    scared the.....out of me.
8. The only way I'm going to get out of
    this financial mess is by finding a.....
    godmother!
9. The Prime Minister is carrying out a witch.....to
    find out who was responsible for the leak.
10. It was supposed to be the holiday of a lifetime
    but it turned out to be hell on.....
11. She's determined to finish the job come hell or
    high.....and nothing you or I say will stop her.
12. He sold his.....to the devil to make her love him
    but it didn't do him any good.
13. Although I can't go with you in person, I'll be
    with you in.....
14. The.....to hell is paved with good intentions.
15. She seems to have cast a.....over him and he's
    like putty in the palm of her hands.

MADAME QIN: WORKSHEET 2 – HOW WELL ARE YOU AGEING?

1. How do you feel about having monkey gland injections to make you look younger?
   a. you're sceptical and doubt if it works
   b. you don't believe in trying to hide your age
   c. you'd be willing to spend everything you had on the treatment
   d. as long as the lines on your face are laughter lines, it really doesn't matter

2. You meet and feel attracted to someone a few years younger. How do you react?
   a. enjoy today but don't expect the relationship to last
   b. see yourself as a father or mother figure
   c. do everything you can to look younger
   d. believe that if the person likes you, he/she will accept you the way you are

3. If someone asked you how many candles they should put on your birthday cake, what would you say?
   a. reply that it's a personal question and refuse to answer
   b. subtract five years c. tell the truth d. pretend you didn't hear

4. You visit your doctor for a check-up and he says that you're fine considering your age. How do you react?
   a. reply with a smile that you're not exactly an antique yet
   b. demand: "What's my age got to do with it?"
   c. start yourself on a punishing keep-fit programme d. feel relieved and thank him

5. How would you feel if a younger person was chosen for a job that you'd applied for?
   a. your qualifications can't have been good enough
   b. it would confirm that firms want younger people
   c. your experience would have made you invaluable to the firm
   d. it would be a waste of time to apply for similar jobs in future

6. You find your first grey hair. What do you do?
   a. pull it out b. dye your hair to make sure it's the last
   c. persuade yourself that grey hair is distinguished
   d. accept that we must all turn grey-haired some time

7. How do you choose your clothes?
   a. to make you look younger b. to follow the latest fashion
   c. to suit your age d. to suit you

8. You're at a party where everyone's younger than you. How do you behave?

a. try to act like everyone else b. just be yourself

c. let your hair down and act young

d. think they might be interested in talking to someone older

9. You meet someone you haven't seen for ages. What remark would you hope for?

a. you haven't changed at all b. I wouldn't have recognized you

c. you look well d. you look as if life's treated you well

10. You're going abroad with someone younger. What do you do?

a. keep your passport hidden b. try to alter the birthdate

c. let them see the passport in case they see it accidentally d. not even give it a thought

ANSWERS

1. a-5 b-3 c-10 d-0	6. a-5 b-10 c-3 d-0
2. a-5 b-3 c-10 d-0	7. a-10 b-5 c-0 d-3
3. a-10 b-5 c-0 d-3	8. a-5 b-0 c-10 d-3
4. a-3 b-5 c-10 d-0	9. a-10 b-5 c-3 d-0
5. a-0 b-5 c-3 d-10	10.a-5 b-10 c-3 d-0

MADAME QIN

Madame Qin was a woman about eighty years old who was in very good health. One day, however, she became very ill and said that she would soon die. She asked her family to gather around her, for she wished to see them one last time. Her little granddaughter, however, lived far away, and it would take five days for her to arrive. No one thought that the woman could wait until her granddaughter's arrival, but she did not die until the girl arrived. After saying a few words to the girl, Madame Qin died. The family was very sad, and the little granddaughter cried herself sick, for she loved her grandmother very much.

Finally the family made preparations for the funeral. However, a strange thing happened on the second day of the ceremonies. Three days after the woman had died, a man suddenly heard a voice from her coffin. It sounded like the cry of a woman, and the man was so afraid that he ran from the coffin. No one dared to go near the coffin except the granddaughter, who said that it must be her grandmother, who was living again. No one believed her, so she went to the coffin and opened it herself. When she did, she saw her grandmother sitting in the coffin. Madame Qin asked why she had been shut up in such a dark box. The girl was so happy that she did not say a word; she just hugged the old woman with tears in her eyes. When everyone came to the room, they were amazed and could not believe what they saw.

The old woman told her family that she had dreamed a very strange dream. She dreamed that she was dead and had come to the land of ghosts. It was a beautiful place, she said. There were flowers all around and many houses in this place. The ghosts lived happily, just as people in this world do. She said that she talked with them, and they told her that they live there very happily and have families. Men have wives and women have husbands. They also have children, but their children were not born to them in our way. They said that when a person in the human world died, she would turn into a baby and come to the ghost world as the child of a couple. Also, when a person in the ghost world died, she would be born to a couple in the human world. They said that a ghost can remember her life in the human world, but a ghost who returns to the human world forgets everything that happened to her before she came to the land of the humans. They also said that they can come to the human world to see their relatives occasionally, but that humans never know about it.

After they told her all of these things, the ghosts took her to visit their king in his palace. The king asked her why she had come to the land of the ghosts. She was very surprised and answered that she had died. Then she asked why she had not turned into a child. The king answered that she had not died and that her time in the human world was not over yet. Then he sent her to a mountain valley and she was scared. Next thing she knew, she awoke and found herself in a dark coffin.

It is said that Madame Qin is still alive today, and that she is in even better health than before.

HEAVEN & HELL

Level: Upper Intermediate
Target Audience: Secondary / Adults
Language / Skills Focus: Listening & Speaking
Materials: Photocopies of the worksheet. Photocopies of the story to hand out at the end of the session (optional).

IN CLASS

1. *Pre-listening:* "They say that the English love their pets more than children. How far do you agree with this?"

2. "When it's time to eat, who would you serve first – your family and friends or your pets? Give reasons for the choice you make."

3. *Post-listening:* "What would heaven on earth be for you and what would hell on earth be for you? Tell the person sitting next to you."

4. Hand out copies of the worksheet and invite the learners to work on the ordering activity and the *True or False* statements in pairs or small groups.

   Match the numbers on the left with the letters on the right to find explanations for the new language in the story: 1-i 2-h 3-c 4-g 5-o 6-m 7-n 8-k 9-b 10-j 11-e 12-d 13-f 14-a 15-l

   True or False: 1. False 2. True 3. True 4. True 5. True 6. True 7. False 8. False

5. *HOW MUCH DO YOU KNOW ABOUT ANIMALS?*
Decide whether the following statements are *True* or *False*:

1. True.
2. True.
3. False. It's actually bright pink.
4. False. They have half the number of taste buds that pigs have.
5. True.
6. False. It's blue.
7. True.
8. True.
9. False. They taste with their feet.
10. True.

COMMENTS

The story, which can be used as a lead-in to work on the topic of Animals, is based on an anecdote in *The Devil and Miss Prym* by Paolo Coelho published by Harper Collins 2001.

HEAVEN AND HELL: WORKSHEET

Match the numbers on the left with the letters on the right to find explanations for the new language in the story:

1.	abandoning	a.	drank until they weren't thirsty any more
2.	apparently	b.	exploit your name
3.	do us a great favour	c.	help us a lot
4.	exhausted	d.	just the opposite
5.	flanked by trees	e.	a movement of the head to indicate yes
6.	heaven	f.	a place where water comes out of the ground
7.	hell	g.	really tired
8.	in the shade of	h.	seemingly
9.	take your name in vain	i.	showing no consideration towards
10.	lightning	j.	a sudden flash of light in the sky during a storm
11.	a nod	k.	under the protection of
12.	on the contrary	l.	walking slowly with heavy steps
13.	a spring	m.	where God is said to live
14.	quenched their thirst	n.	where the Devil is said to live
15.	trudging	o.	with trees on either side

True or False
1. A man, a horse and his dog died when they were hit by lightning.
2. They were thirsty because the weather was hot and they had to climb up a hill.
3. The guard at the marble gateway lied to the man when he asked for the name of the place.
4. The man wouldn't drink from the fountain because the animals weren't allowed to drink there.
5. The journey to the old gateway was also uphill.
6. The man and his animals all drank from the spring.
7. The first place the man visited was Heaven and the second place was Hell.
8. People who mistreated their animals were welcomed in the second place.

HOW MUCH DO YOU KNOW ABOUT ANIMALS?

Decide whether the following statements are *True* or *False*:

1. A giraffe can survive longer without water than a camel.
2. A crocodile has so much acid in its stomach that it can even digest steel.
3. Hippopotamus milk is bright blue in colour.
4. Humans have around 8,000 taste buds, twice the number of taste buds that pigs have.
5. The creature with the best hearing is probably the owl. It can hear a mouse stepping on a twig 20 metres away.
6. The tongue of a giraffe is green in colour.
7. Birds of prey have the best eyesight and can spot a small rodent on the ground when they are flying at more than 15,000ft.
8. The tongue of a blue whale weighs as much as a full-grown African elephant.
9. Butterflies taste with their noses.
10. The anopheles mosquito, which carries malaria, is believed to have been responsible for half of all human deaths - barring wars and accidents - since the Stone Age.

HEAVEN & HELL

Once upon a time, a man, his horse and his dog were travelling along a road. As they passed by a huge tree, it was struck by lightning and they all died. But the man didn't realize that he was dead so he continued walking with his two animal companions, just as before.

It was a long, uphill walk, the sun was beating down on them and they were all hot and thirsty. At a bend in the road they saw a magnificent marble gateway that led into a gold-paved square. And in the centre of the square was a fountain overflowing with crystal-clear water.

"Good morning. What is this place?"

"It's Heaven," the guard at the entrance replied.

"Well I'm very glad to see it, I can tell you, because we're extremely thirsty."

"You're welcome to come in and drink all the water you want."

"My horse and dog need water too."

"I'm terribly sorry," said the guard, "but animals are not allowed in here."

Although the man was really thirsty, he was not prepared to drink alone. So he thanked the guard and went on his way. Exhausted after more trudging uphill, they eventually reached an old gateway that opened on to a dirt road flanked by trees. A man, his hat pulled down over his face, was stretched out in the shade of one of the trees, apparently asleep.

"Good morning," said the traveller.

The other man greeted him with a nod.

"We're very thirsty – me, my horse and my dog."

"There's a spring over there amongst those rocks," said the man indicating the spot. You can drink as much as you want."

So they went to the spring, quenched their thirst and the traveller then returned to thank the man.

"By the way, what's this place called?"

"Heaven."

"Heaven. But the guard at the marble gateway told me that was Heaven!"

"That's not Heaven, that's Hell."

The traveller was puzzled.

"You shouldn't let others take your name in vain, you know! False information can lead to all kinds of confusion!"

"On the contrary, they do us a great favour. The ones who stay there are those who have proved themselves capable of abandoning their dearest friends and have no place here anyway."

WHY THERE IS NIGHT

Level: Elementary
Target Audience: Secondary / Adults
Language / Skills Focus: Listening & Speaking, Past Simple - regular and irregular verbs
Materials: Photocopies of the worksheet

IN CLASS

1. *Pre-listening:* Match the numbers on the left with the letters on the right: 1-b 2-h 3-a 4-e 5-i 6-g 7-f 8-d 9-c

2. *Post-listening:* Listen to the story, and then use each of the following verbs once only to complete the text: 1. were   2. was 3. had 4.laughed 5. complained 6. answered 7. ordered 8. got 9. picked 10. threw

3. Which of the verbs in the text are regular and which of the verbs are irregular? And how can you tell? (The Past Simple of a regular verb is formed by adding ED to the root).

4. In the story the Moon laughs at the Sun because he does the cooking. Whose job is it to do the cooking – a man's job or a woman's? And are there some jobs only for men and other jobs only for women? Working in small groups, discuss these questions:

COMMENTS

The story is a Creation Myth from the Philippines and was taken from *ELT through Multiple Intelligences* by Michael Berman, Netlearn Publications 2001.

THE STORY

Once upon a time the Sun and the Moon were both very bright and it was always daytime.

The Sun had no wife so the Moon laughed at him. "Why are you always laughing at me?" The Sun complained. "I'm getting very tired of you."

The Moon answered "I'm laughing at you because you have no wife and you must cook your food yourself. A God who cooks his own food! Ha! Ha! Ha!"

"Stop laughing at me at once!" The Sun ordered. "The problem with you is that you have no respect." But the Moon didn't stop laughing and the Sun got very angry. He picked up a handful of coals from his fire and he threw them into the Moon's face.

So now the Moon can't shine so brightly and he hides for half the day because he's ashamed of his appearance. And that's how we have day and night.

WHY THERE IS NIGHT: WORKSHEET

Match the numbers on the left with the letters on the right:

1.	bright	a.	how you feel after your English class perhaps!
2.	to laugh	b.	sunny
3.	tired	c.	the way something looks
4.	to complain	d.	to be embarrassed by
5.	respect	e.	to show you're not happy with something
6.	coals	f.	what the sun does
7.	to shine	g.	you can use these to make a fire
8.	to be ashamed of	h.	you do this when something is funny
9.	appearance	i.	you should have this for people older than you

Why isn't it light 24 hours a day and why do we have night? The story you're going to hear explains the reason and it comes from the Philippines. Listen to the story, and then use each of the following verbs once only to complete the text: answered / complained / got / had / laughed / ordered / picked / threw / was / were

Once upon a time the Sun and the Moon 1. _____ both very bright and it 2. _____ always daytime.

The Sun 3. _____ no wife so the Moon 4. _____ at him. "Why are you always laughing at me?" The Sun 5. _____. "I'm getting very tired of you."

The Moon 6. _____ "I'm laughing at you because you have no wife and you must cook your food yourself. A God who cooks his own food! Ha! Ha! Ha!"

"Stop laughing at me at once!" The Sun 7. _____. "The problem with you is that you have no respect." But the Moon didn't stop laughing and the Sun 8. _____ very angry. He 9. _____ up a handful of coals from his fire and he 10. _____ them into the Moon's face.

So now the Moon can't shine so brightly and he hides for half the day because he's ashamed of his appearance. And that's how we have day and night.

Which of the verbs in the text are regular and which of the verbs are irregular? And how can you tell?

In the story the Moon laughs at the Sun because he does the cooking. Whose job is it to do the cooking – a man's job or a woman's? And are there some jobs only for men and other jobs only for women? Working in small groups, discuss these questions:

THE UNHAPPIEST PERSON IN THE WORLD

Level: Intermediate / Upper Intermediate

Target Audience: Secondary, Adults

Language / Skills Focus: Listening & Predicting

Materials: Photocopies of the story (optional) to hand out to the learners after the telling of the tale

IN CLASS

1   Start with a brainstorming session to find out what advice the learners would offer to someone suffering from depression. They can then listen to the tale to see whether their suggestions feature in it.

2   Alternatively, ask the learners to find the answers to the following questions while listening to the tale. They can be written up on the board beforehand or presented on an OHT.

a. What was the patient's problem?

b. Who did he turn to as a last resort?

c. What were the four suggestions he made?

d. Why did the first three suggestions turn out to be unhelpful?

After telling the story and checking the answers to the questions, arrange the students into groups of four to predict the ending. Ask a spokesperson from each group to present their suggestions to the class before providing the missing line. (The missing line is " ….. I am the Great Delmonte!")

Now invite the learners, working on their own, to each make a list with all the reasons they have for being happy today (You might like to set a time limit for this. For example, "You have as long as this piece of music lasts to make a list with all the reasons you have for being happy today"). They can then pair up, or form small groups, to share their good news.

COMMENTS

The idea for this story was taken from an anecdote in *The Active Side of Infinity* by Carlos Castaneda, Harper Collins 1998.

THE UNHAPPIEST PERSON IN THE WORLD

Once upon a time there was a man who suffered from severe depression. He went to see the best doctors in the land for money was no object but nobody seemed able to help him. In desperation, as a last resort, he then turned to a leading practitioner of complimentary medicine.

After listening in detail to the patient's description of his symptoms, the doctor suggested that the patient could find solace, and the end of his suffering, in love. The man, however, responded that love had never been a problem for him and that he was loved perhaps like nobody else in the world.

The doctor then suggested travelling and seeing other parts of the world. However, the poor miserable soul responded, without exaggeration, he had already been everywhere and seen everything there was to see.

"Then how about taking up a new hobby? Something completely different to anything you've ever done before. That should do the trick." But it turned out that the patient had tried that too and found no relief.

The doctor began to suspect that the man was an incurable liar. How could he possibly have done all the things he claimed? But being a good healer, the doctor had a final insight.

"Not to worry. I have the perfect solution for you, sir. You must attend a performance of the greatest comedian of our day. He will amuse you to such an extent that you will be cured forever. You must attend a performance of the Great Delmonte."

The man looked at the doctor with the saddest look you can possibly imagine. If that's your recommendation doctor, then I am truly a lost man and there is no cure for my condition because

---

Make a list with all the reasons you have for being happy today. Then find yourself a partner to share your good news with!

THE TAIL OF THE DOG

Level: Intermediate
Target Audience: Secondary, Adults
Language / Skills Focus: Listening, Speaking & Writing
Materials: Photocopies of the worksheet

IN CLASS

As a pre-listening activity, start with a brainstorming session: *Why do dogs have tails?*

As a post-listening activity, hand out copies of the worksheet with the questionnaire. This can be completed individually or in groups. The answers are presented below:

1. The order you chose represents your priorities in life: Cow signifies career, tiger signifies pride, sheep signifies love, horse signifies family, and pig signifies money.

2. Your description of the dog is how you see your own personality, your description of the cat is what you think of your partner, your description of the rat is how you see your enemies, your description of coffee is how you feel about sex, and your description of the Sea is how you see your own life.

3. Yellow is for someone you will never forget, orange for someone you consider to be your true friend, red for someone that you really love, white for your soul mate, and green for someone that you will remember for the rest of your life.

    Arrange the learners into groups and invite them to work on parallel stories. They can make use of the suggested titles below. While this is taking place, circulate to provide any assistance required. Then invite a spokesperson for each group to read their tale to the rest of the class:

    The Trunk of the Elephant / The Neck of the Giraffe / The Horn of the Rhinoceros / The Sting of the Bee etc. etc.

4. If there is any time left at the end of the lesson, the following question could be discussed: *What other disastrous consequences can there be for people who have big mouths?*

COMMENTS

Fables are sources of metaphor and provide vehicles to create, recreate, and preserve culture. The example presented here, *The Tail of the Dog*, is adapted from a story written by Maya author and archaeologist Victor Montejo. The tail was the dog's punishment for not being able to recognize where the boundaries lay.

THE TAIL OF THE DOG: WORKSHEET

Of the origins of the world only the dog could speak. He went around everywhere, revealing the secret of the creation of things and the origin of God.

And when the Creator realized the talkative dog could not hold his tongue and keep the secrets, he made the following decision: "Let this talker's marvellous tongue be taken from his head and put it behind him, and let what is now behind him, be attached to his head."

So it is now that when the dog wants to speak and tell things, no expression appears on its face but there it is behind him, the tail that came from his head.

And so the dog has stayed with us - he who once betrayed God's secrets. And even now, he only moves his tail when he wants to tell us something or when he's happy with his master.

WHAT KIND OF PERSON ARE YOU?

1. Put the following 5 animals in the order of your preference.
   a. Cow
   b. Tiger
   c. Sheep
   d. Horse
   e. Pig

2. Write one word that describes each of the following:
   a. Dog
   b. Cat
   c. Rat
   d. Coffee
   e. Sea

3. Who do you associate the following colours with? For each colour choose someone different, someone important to you who knows you well.
   a. Yellow
   b. Orange
   c. Red
   d. White
   e. Green

THE FOOD OF THE CLOAK

Level: Intermediate – Advanced
Target Audience: Secondary / Adults
Language / Skills Focus: Listening & Speaking
Materials: Photocopies of the worksheet

IN CLASS

1. *Pre-Listening:* They say you shouldn't judge people by appearances but what do you think? How important do you consider clothes to be? The tale that follows shows how misleading the way someone dresses can be.

2. *Post-listening*: Match the numbers on the left with the letters on the right: 1-i / 2-b / 3-a / 4-c / 5-d/ 6-g / 7-h / 8-f/ 9-e

3. FOOD & DRINK IDIOMS: 1 peas 2 cherry 3 potato 4 meat 5 onions 6 jelly 7 sauce 8 fruitcake 9 pudding 10 tea 11 fish 12 mustard 13 chicken 14 cake 15 apple

COMMENTS

Many teaching stories come from Sufi sources and are about a character called Mullah Nasrudin. Although several nations of the Middle East claim the Mullah as their own, like all mythological characters he belongs to everyone. The Mullah is a wise fool and his stories have many meanings on multiple levels of reality. The stories show that things are not always as they appear and often logic fails us.

THE FOOD OF THE CLOAK: WORKSHEET

They say that you shouldn't judge people by appearances but what do you think? How important do you consider clothes to be?

Match the numbers on the left with the letters on the right to find explanations of the new language in the story:

1.	a cloak	a.	a head covering worn by Muslims.
2.	a feast	b.	a special meal
3.	a turban	c.	a very important person
4.	a visitor of high rank	d.	I'm interested in finding out about
5.	I am curious as to	e.	immediately
6.	inconspicuous	f.	looked after very well
7.	ragged	g.	not easily noticed
8.	waited on hand and foot	h.	old and torn
9.	Without a pause	i.	something you wear over your shoulders instead of a coat

FOOD+DRINK IDIOMS Use the following words to complete the sentences below. One of the words you will need to use twice: apple / chicken / jelly / onions / pudding / cake / fish / meat / peas / sauce / cherry / fruitcake / mustard / potato / tea

1. It's hardly surprising that they get on so well together - they're as alike as two _____ in a pod.
2. You'd better make the most of the opportunity because you won't get two bites at the _____.
3. When she found out that he was a married man, she dropped him like a hot. _____.
4. The job might suit you but it doesn't suit me - one man's _____ is another man's poison.
5. He clearly knows his _____ and it's obvious that he's an expert in the field.
6. What are you so nervous about? You're shaking like a _____!
7. If it's suitable for you, then it's suitable for me - what's _____ for the goose is _____ for the gander.
8. I don't believe a word you're telling me and I think you're as nutty as a _____!
9. It seems a good idea in theory but the proof of the _____ is in the eating.
10. Rap music is popular with a lot of young people but it's not my cup of _____.
11. I wasn't able to go to the party because I had other _____ to fry.
12. I can see that you're as keen as _____ on studying the language so you should make rapid progress.
13. I can't understand what he's complaining about - his rent is _____ feed in comparison with mine.
14. She needn't have worried about the exam - it turned out to be a piece of _____.
15. They say an _____ a day keeps the doctor away but I think it's an old wives' tail!

THE FOOD OF THE CLOAK

Mulla Nasrudin heard that there was a party being held in the nearby town, and that everyone was invited. He made his way there as quickly as he could. When the Master of the Ceremonies saw him in his ragged cloak, he seated him in the most inconspicuous place, far from the great table where the most important people were being waited on hand and foot.

Mulla saw that it would be at least an hour before the waiters reached the place he was sitting. So he got up and went home.

He dressed himself in a magnificent sable cloak and turban and returned to the feast. As soon as the herald of the Emir, his host, saw this splendid sight they started to beat the drum of welcome and sound the trumpets in a manner consonant with a visitor of high rank.

The Chamberlain came out of the palace himself, and conducted the magnificent Nasrudin to a place almost next to the Emir. A dish of wonderful food was immediately placed before him. Without a pause, Nasrudin began to rub handfuls of it into his turban and cloak.

"Your eminence," said the prince, "I am curious as to your eating habits, which are new to me."

"Nothing special," said Mulla, "the cloak got me here, got me the food. Surely it deserves its share!"

WIFE FOR A WALRUS, LORD OF THE SEA

Level: Advanced
Target Audience: Adults
Language / Skills Focus: Listening & Speaking
Materials: Photocopies of the worksheet. Photocopies of the story (optional) to hand out at the end of the session.

IN CLASS

1. *Pre-listening:* Start with a brainstorming session. *What do you know about walruses?*

2. *While-listening:* Pause after "they saw at once that all was not as it should be" and ask the learners to predict what the problem was.

3. Pause after "she vanished into thin air" and ask the class to predict what had happened to her.

4. Pause after "From this day on I must ..." and ask the learners to predict what follows.

5. *Post-listening:* Read through the story to find words which mean the same as the following: a. had to make do with / b. How can I go home empty-handed? / c. He sat there sorrowing for a long time / d. Having eaten their fill / e. all was not as it should be / f. They looked high and low / g. but to no avail / h. she vanished into the air / i. A great trembling seized the old man / j. she mustn't grieve for me. / k. From this day on, neither of you shall want for anything

6. Working in small groups. Discuss the following questions. Elect a spokesperson to take notes and present your views to the rest of the class:
    a. Why do you think the woman hid the sabre in the chest?
    b. What do you think the father would have preferred – to have had as much food as he needed for the rest of his life or to have had his daughter back?
    c. What other stories about mermaids or mermen do you know?
    d. Have you ever been in a situation where you did not have enough food to eat and were constantly hungry? How did you manage? Tell me about it.

COMMENTS

Wife for a Walrus, Lord of the Sea has been adapted from a Siberian folktale in *The Sun Maiden and The Crescent Moon* by James Riordan, Interlink Books 1991. The story can be used as a lead-in to work on the topic of *The Supernatural*.

WIFE FOR A WALRUS, LORD OF THE SEA

There was once an old man and his wife who were very poor. In fact, they were so poor that they never knew the smell of good food and had to make do with the putrid fish cast up on the shore.

Now the old pair had a daughter who grew up to be very beautiful. And the young girl lived with her parents, hungered with them and, like them, ate whatever the sea might yield.

Late one winter the family remained without a scrap of food and did not know what to do. Every day the old man went down to the shore in the hope of finding dead fish or a rotting carcass of a seal, but though he wandered far along the beach he found nothing. Finally, he sat down upon a large rock, his head in his hands.

"How can I go home empty-handed?" he sighed. "What will I feed my wife and daughter on?"

He sat there sorrowing for a long time, and when at twilight he had to leave, he cast a last hopeful glance at the sea. It had suddenly turned dark and menacing, then began to seethe and boil like water in a cauldron.

In awe he watched from behind the rock as the waves flung a huge whale upon the shore. All at once six great walruses, lords of the sea, leapt out in pursuit. They cut the whale to pieces with their sabres and then vanished back into the sea.

Once all was still again, the old man crept fearfully up to the dead whale and there, beside him, found a sabre left by the walruses.

"What a rich present the sea has brought me!" He was overjoyed.

Picking up the sabre, he cut a good slice of meat from the whale and went home. He handed the meat and the sabre to his wife who immediately hid the sabre in a large chest, then cooked the meat to feed her family.

Having eaten their fill, the old man and woman lay down to sleep. They slept soundly and it was past dawn by the time they awoke. Glancing round, they saw at once that all was not as it should be: their daughter was missing.

"Where has our child gone?" they cried in alarm. And as soon as the sun was up they set about searching for the girl. They looked high and low throughout the day until it was quite dark, but to no avail. When they came back to their choom, however, there was their daughter sitting at the entrance looking up at them sadly.

"Where have you been, my child?" the old woman asked.

The daughter said nothing but was clearly upset.

The three of them went inside, yet none could sleep or talk. As they sat in silence, the daughter abruptly rose and made to leave the choom. No sooner had she stepped through the opening than she vanished into the air.

Spring followed winter in due course without her having returned and one day, while on the shore looking for fish, the old man found himself by the rock he had sat on the previous year. Now he sat on it again and gazed out to sea, thinking all the while of his dear daughter and wishing with all his heart that he could see her once more.

"Come to me, my child," he whispered. "Come to your old father, wherever you are, even from the depths of the sea."

And as he gazed into the waters, he saw that the sea had turned dark and menacing. It seethed and boiled like water in a cauldron, just as it had done once before. Then six giant walruses, lords of the sea, rose from the depths on the crest of a wave and there, sitting on the back of the biggest, was his daughter.

A great trembling seized the old man; he began to weep and cry, saying over and over again:

"Oh, my child, my only child! You've come to me from the bottom of the sea. Won't you speak me?"

"I will, Father, I will!" the daughter replied. "Listen carefully to what I have to say: you angered the lords of the sea by taking their sabre and I've been made to pay for it. Go home and tell my mother of the punishment and return to this rock in a year."

With that she vanished back into the sea, and the old man went home to tell his wife the news.

A year passed, spring came once more and the old man hurried down to the shore. Sitting on the self-same rock, he fixed his gaze upon the sea.

"Come to me, my child," he called softly. "Come to me, wherever you are, even from the bottom of the sea."

All at once, a huge wave struck the shore, and out of the depths came a giant walrus, the Lord of the Sea himself, with the old man's beautiful daughter on his back. She stepped gently down and stood before her father. The old man looked and could hardly believe what his eyes saw.

For there stood his daughter, more radiant than ever, her dark hair almost to her waist, and in her arms lay a smiling baby. The young mother was holding the baby for her father to see.

"Come here no more, Father," she told him, "for I can never return. I'm the wife of the Lord of the Sea now and have borne him this son. From this day on I must remain with him. Tell my mother that I'm content and that she mustn't grieve for me. From this day on, neither of you shall want for anything. Should you desire meat, come to the shore and you shall find it. I shall send as many seals as you wish and you shall never be short of food again."

With that she climbed on the walrus's back and he plunged back into the depths. He and the girl with her baby disappeared, and the old man turned for home.

As the daughter had promised, so it was. The old man and woman lived on for a good many years and came to know the taste of good food for the rest of their lives. Yet never again did they see their dear daughter.

WIFE FOR A WALRUS, LORD OF THE SEA: WORKSHEET

Read through the story to find words which mean the same as the following:

a.   needed to manage with nothing more than

b.   How can I return without any food?

c.   He remained there feeling miserable for ages

d.   Having satisfied their hunger

e.   something was clearly wrong

f.   They searched absolutely everywhere

g.   but without any luck

h.   she disappeared without a trace

i.   The old man was overcome with sadness

j.   not to feel sorry for me

k.   You will both never go short of food again

Discuss the following questions in small groups. Elect a spokesperson to take notes and present your views to the rest of the class:

a.   Why do you think the woman hid the sabre in the chest?
b.   What do you think the father would have preferred – to have had as much food as he needed for the rest of his life or to have had his daughter back?
c.   What other stories about mermaids or mermen do you know?
d.   Have you ever been in a situation where you did not have enough food to eat and were constantly hungry? How did you manage? Tell me about it.

GOLD-TREE AND SILVER-TREE

Level: Intermediate – Advanced
Target Audience: Secondary
Language / Skills Focus: Listening & Role Play
Materials: Photocopies of the worksheet. Photocopies of the story (optional) to hand out at the end of the session.

IN CLASS

1 As a pre-listening activity, elicit what fairy tales are and how they usually start and finish. (Once upon a time and they all lived happily ever after) Ask the students if they can name or tell you any. They will probably be familiar with the story of *Sleeping Beauty* and this is an early Celtic version of it.

2 During the while-listening stage, there are several opportunities to ask the learners to anticipate what follows:

Pause after "Troutie, bonny little fellow, am I not the most beautiful queen in the world?" Ask the students to predict what happens next: What do you expect the trout's answer to be?

Pause after "so that your own mother may give a kiss to it" Ask the class to predict what follows: What do you think happens next?

Pause after "What gift ..... would you give me that I could make you laugh?" Ask the students to predict the answer: How do you think the Prince is going to answer the question?

3 It seems that the Prince lived happily ever after with both wives together. Do you think it's possible to be in love with two people at the same time? Would you be happy to share your partner with someone else? These questions could lead into a discussion.

4 Read through the story to find words which mean the same as the following: a. a well / b. blind with rage / c. vowed / d. only a thing which you may heal if you like / e. he was in great sorrow / f. In the course of time he married again / g. looking very downcast / h. he made great rejoicings

5 Arrange the students in groups of three. The Prince has decided that the time has come to make a choice between his two wives. Student A plays the part of the Prince and interviews his two wives - B and C. The wives should try to justify why they deserve to be chosen and the Prince then makes his choice!

6   The *Tree Idioms* exercise on the worksheet is intended for higher level students and could be set for homework: 1. branch 2. tree 3. bark 4. root 5. leaf 6. stick 7. rooted 8. roots 9. wood / trees 10. trees 11. wood 12. wood / leaf 13. bush 14. paper

GOLD-TREE AND SILVER-TREE: WORKSHEET

Read through the story to find words which mean the same as the following:

a. a deep hole in the ground that provides water

b. absolutely furious

c. made a serious promise

d. something only you can help me to recover from

e. he was bitterly upset

f. eventually he found another wife

g. appearing to be very miserable

h. he showed the world how happy he was

ROLE PLAY Work in groups of three. The Prince has decided that the time has come to make a choice between his two wives. Student A plays the part of the Prince and interviews his two wives - B and C. The wives should try to justify why they deserve to be chosen and the Prince then makes his choice!

TREE IDIOMS Use the following words to complete the sentences below:

    bark / leaf / roots / trees
    branch / paper / stick / wood
    bush / root / tree / wood
    leaf / rooted / trees / wood

1. Instead of working for someone else, why don't you _____ out on your own?
2. It's no good blaming me for what happened - you're barking up the wrong _____.
3. Don't let the Director frighten you – her _____ is worse than her bite!
4. They say that money is the _____ of all evil but I'm not sure I agree.
5. What are you in such a state about? You're shaking like a _____!
6. I'm afraid there's been a misunderstanding and you've got hold of the wrong end of the

    _____

7. He caught such a fright when he saw the snake that he stood _____ to the spot.
8. I feel that this year is a time for putting down _____ and consolidating what I have.
9. It's such a complex issue that it's difficult to see the _____ for the _____.
10. You spend money like it's going out of fashion - it doesn't grow on _____ you know!
11. Although we have managed to reduce our losses since last year, we are still not out of the

    _____ yet.

12. The astrologer told me that I need to cut the dead _____ out of my life and to turn over a

    new _____.

13. Instead of beating around the _____, I'd appreciate it if you got straight to the point.
14. Although they tried to _____ over the cracks, it was clear that their marriage was on the

    rocks.

GOLD-TREE AND SILVER-TREE

Once upon a time there was a king who had a wife, whose name was Silver-tree, and a daughter, whose name was Gold-tree. On a certain day of the days, Gold-tree and Silver-tree went to a glen, where there was a well, and in it there was a trout.

Said Silver-tree, "Troutie, bonny little fellow, am not I the most beautiful queen in the world?"

"Oh! indeed you are not."

"Who then?"

"Why, Gold-tree, your daughter."

Silver-tree went home, blind with rage. She lay down on the bed, and vowed she would never be well until she could get the heart and the liver of Gold-tree, her daughter, to eat.

At nightfall the king came home, and it was told him that Silver-tree, his wife, was very ill. He went where she was, and asked her what was wrong with her.

"Oh!" only a thing which you may heal if you like."

"Oh!" indeed there is nothing at all which I could do for you that I would not do."

"If I get the heart and the liver of Gold-tree, my daughter, to eat, I shall be well."

Now it happened about this time that the son of a great king had come from abroad to ask Goldtree for marrying. The king now agreed to this, and they went abroad.

The king then went and sent his lads to the hunting-hill for a he-goat, and he gave its heart and its liver to his wife to eat; and she rose well and healthy.

A year after this Silver-tree went to the glen, where there was the well in which there was the trout.

"Troutie, bonny little fellow," said she, "am not I the most beautiful queen in the world?"

"Oh! indeed you are not."

"Who, then?"

"Why, Gold-tree, your daughter."

"Oh! well, it is long since she was living. It is a year since I ate her heart and liver."

"Oh! indeed she is not dead. She is married to a great prince abroad."

Silver-tree went home, and begged the king to put the long-ship in order, and said, "I am going to see my dear Gold-tree, for it is so long since I saw her." The long-ship was put in order, and they went away.

It was Silver-tree herself that was at the helm, and she steered the ship so well that they were not long at all before they arrived.

The prince was out hunting on the hills. Gold-tree knew the long-ship of her father coming. "Oh!" said she to the servants, "my mother is coming, and she will kill me."

"She shall not kill you at all; we will lock you in a room where she cannot get near you."

This is how it was done; and when Silver-tree came ashore, she began to cry out:

"Come to meet your own mother, when she comes to see you." Gold-tree said that she could not, that she was locked in the room, and that she could not get out of it.

"Will you not put out," said Silver-tree, "your little finger through the key -hole, so that your own mother may give a kiss to it?"

She put out her little finger, and Silver-tree went and put a poisoned stab in it, and Gold-tree fell dead.

When the prince came home, and found Gold-tree dead, he was in great sorrow, and when he saw how beautiful she was, he did not bury her at all, but he locked her in a room where nobody would get near her.

In the course of time he married again, and the whole house was under the hand of this wife but one room, and he himself always kept the key of that room. On a certain day of the days he forgot to take the key with him, and the second wife got into the room. What did she see there but the most beautiful woman that she ever saw.

She began to turn and try to wake her, and she noticed the poisoned stab in her finger. She took the stab out, and Gold-tree rose alive, as beautiful as she was ever.

At the fall of night the prince came home from the hunting-hill, looking very downcast.

"What gift," said his wife, "would you give me that I could make you laugh?"

"Oh! indeed, nothing could make me laugh, except Gold-tree were to come alive again."
"Well, you'll find her alive down there in the room."

When the prince saw Gold-tree alive he made great rejoicings, and he began to kiss her, and kiss her, and kiss her. Said the second wife, "Since she is the first one you had it is better for you to stick to her, and I will go away."

"Oh! indeed you shall not go away, but I shall have both of you."

At the end of the year, Silver-tree went to the glen, where there was the well, in which there was the trout.

"Troutie, bonny little fellow," said she, "am not I the most beautiful queen in the world?"

"Oh! indeed you are not."

"Who then?"

"Why, Gold-tree, your daughter."

"Oh! well, she is not alive. It is a year since I put the poisoned stab into her finger."

"Oh! indeed she is not dead at all, at all."

Silver-tree went home, and begged the king to put the long-ship in order, for that she was going to see her dear Gold-tree, as it was so long since she saw her. The long-ship was put in order, and they went away. It was Silver-tree herself that was at the helm, and she steered the ship so well that they were not long at all before they arrived.

The prince was out hunting on the hills. Gold-tree knew her father's ship coming.

"Oh!" said she, "my mother is coming, and she will kill me."

"Not at all," said the second wife; "we will go down to meet her."

Silver-tree came ashore. "Come down, Gold-tree, love," said she, "for your own mother has come to you with a precious drink."

"It is a custom in this country," said the second wife, "that the person who offers a drink takes a draught out of it first."

Silver-tree put her mouth to it, and the second wife went and struck it so that some of it went down her throat, and she fell dead. They only had to carry her home a dead corpse and bury her.

The prince and his two wives were long alive after this, pleased and peaceful. I left them there.

(taken from "Celtic Fairy Tales" collected by Joseph Jacobs - 1968 Dover Publications Inc. 180 Varick Street New York NY 10014)

THE DOG THAT WENT ABROAD

Level: Upper Intermediate
Target Audience: Adults
Language / Skills Focus: Listening, Speaking & Letter Writing
Materials: An OHP with the pre-listening questions for pair-work. (If you do not have access to an OHT, you can board these questions before the start of the class instead). Photocopies of the worksheet. Photocopies of the story (optional) to hand out at the end of the session.

IN CLASS

1. *Pre-listening:* Working in pairs, take it in turns ask each other the following questions, then report back to the rest of the class with your findings:

    a. Have your experiences on your travels been positive, negative or a bit of both?

    b. What's the most important lesson you've learnt from your travels?

    c. Before we travel, we have expectations about the places we're going to visit. Tell me about a place you've been to that was totally different to what you expected it to be.

2. *While-listening:* Pause after "There's only one evil in a foreign country:" and ask the learners to predict the ending.

3. *Post-listening:* Place the nine parts of the story in the correct order 1-c / 2-a / 3-f / 4-b / 5-e / 6-i / 7-h / 8-d / 9-g

4. Match the numbers on the left with the letters on the right to find explanations for the new vocabulary: 1-e / 2-f / 3-d / 4-h / 5-c / 6-a / 7-i / 8-g / 9-b

5. When you get back home from your travels, what will you tell all your relatives and friends about your experience of living in a foreign country? And if you are studying English in your own country rather than abroad, then invent what you would tell them about in that situation. You could do this in the form of a letter, either in class or for homework. (You might like to brainstorm how to lay out an informal letter with the learners before setting this task).

COMMENTS

The Dog that went Abroad is based on a story from *The Panchatantra*, five books of animal fables and magic tales from India that were compiled between the third and fifth centuries AD. It is believed that even then the stories were already ancient. Although the original author is unknown, an Arabic translation from about 750 AD attributes *The Panchatantra* to a wise man called *Bidpai*, which is probably a Sanskrit word meaning "court scholar." The story can be used as a lead-in to work on the topic of *Travelling*.

THE DOG THAT WENT ABROAD

In a certain place there once lived a dog by the name of Tschitranga, which means "having a spotted body." A lengthy famine set in. Because they had no food, the dogs and other animals began to leave their families. Tschitranga, who was emaciated with hunger, was driven by fear to another country. There in a certain city he went to a certain house day after day where, due to the carelessness of the housekeeper, many good things to eat were left lying about, and he ate his fill. However, when he left the house, other vicious dogs surrounded him on all sides and tore into him on all parts of his body with their teeth. Then he reconsidered his situation, and said, "I've come to the conclusion that it really is better at home. Even during a famine you can live there in peace, and no one bites you to pieces. I'm going to return to my own city."

When he got back home, all of his relatives were curious about his travels and asked him lots of questions. "Tschitranga, tell us about where you've been. What's the country like? How do the people behave? What do they eat? What do they do?"

He answered, "How can I explain to you the essence of a foreign place? There are good things to eat in great variety, and housekeepers who don't keep watch! There's only one evil in a foreign country: You'll be hated there because of who you are!"

THE DOG THAT WENT ABROAD: WORKSHEET

Place the nine parts of the story in the correct order:

a. Because they had no food, the dogs and other animals began to leave their families. Tschitranga, who was emaciated with hunger, was driven by fear to another country.

b. However, when he left the house, other vicious dogs surrounded him on all sides and tore into him on all parts of his body with their teeth.

c. In a certain place there once lived a dog by the name of Tschitranga, which means "having a spotted body." A lengthy famine set in.

d. He answered, "How can I explain to you the essence of a foreign place? There are good things to eat in great variety, and housekeepers who don't keep watch!

e. Then he reconsidered his situation, and said, "I've come to the conclusion that it really is better at home. Even during a famine you can live there in peace, and no one bites you to pieces. I'm going to return to my own city."

f. There in a certain city he went to a certain house day after day where, due to the carelessness of the housekeeper, many good things to eat were left lying about, and he ate his fill.

g. There's only one evil in a foreign country: You'll be hated there because of who you are!"

h. "Tschitranga, tell us about where you've been. What's the country like? How do the people behave? What do they eat? What do they do?"

i. When he got back home, all his relatives were curious about his travels and asked him lots of questions.

ANSWERS: 1 _____ 2 _____ 3 _____ 4 _____ 5 _____ 6 _____ 7 _____ 8 _____ 9 _____

Match the numbers on the left with the letters on the right to find explanations for the new vocabulary:

1.	lengthy	a.	ate until he wasn't hungry any more
2.	famine	b.	bad thing
3.	set in	c.	because of
4.	emaciated	d.	established itself
5.	due to	e.	lasting a long time
6.	ate his fill	f.	a long period of time with no food
7.	vicious	g.	the basic, most important part
8.	essence	h.	very thin and weak
9.	evil (noun)	i.	violent and dangerous

When you get back home from your travels, what will you tell all your relatives and friends about your experience of living in a foreign country? And if you are studying English in your own country rather than abroad, then imagine what you will tell them about. You could do this in the form of a letter, either in class or for homework.

FAITHFUL EVEN IN DEATH

Level: Upper Intermediate – Advanced
Target Audience: Secondary / Adults
Language / Skills Focus: Listening, Speaking & Writing
Materials: Photocopies of the worksheet. Photocopies of the story (optional) to hand out at the end of the session.

IN CLASS

1   *Pre-listening:* What would you do if you wanted to marry someone your parents didn't approve of? Would you follow your heart or respect your parents' wishes? Arrange the learners in small groups to discuss the question and to see if they can reach an agreement.

2   In the past, young people often had no choice as marriages were arranged. In fact, they still are today in some countries. How do you feel about arranged marriages? Are they more or less likely to be successful? What do you think? Today's story is all about an arranged marriage that took place in China.

3   *Post-listening:* "Are You Ruled By Your Heart Or Your Head?" After pre-teaching new vocabulary, arrange the students in groups. Hand out a copy of the questionnaire to an "interviewer" in each group who reads the questions to the other students and takes on the role of the teacher. Only the interviewer should be able to see the copy and he/she presents the questionnaire to the group as a listening activity. Meanwhile, you can circulate to provide any assistance required. The next stage is for the learners to add up their scores and assess the results, which can be examined and discussed by the class as a whole. Although the material is inauthentic in that the questionnaire is contrived, the students have an authentic reason for doing the activity - to find out more about themselves.

4   Write an account of (or tell the other people in your group about) a love story with a happy ending - real or imaginary.

FAITHFUL EVEN IN DEATH: WORKSHEET

Are you ruled by your Heart or your Head?

1. What would you rather be known as?
    a. a sympathetic person
    b. an intelligent person

2. Which qualities do you value in a friend?
    a. support and love
    b. common sense and practical advice

3. When can you tell you're in love?
    a. when you realise someone has the qualities you're looking for
    b. when you heart beats faster and you go weak at the knees

4. Which bits do you like best when reading a newspaper?
    a. the news and the crossword
    b. romantic short stories and the "agony aunt" page

5. What do you believe we should teach children?
    a. how to listen to other people
    b. how to win arguments

6. What's your favourite kind of music?
    a. poetic and intellectual
    b. sentimental and romantic

7. What sort of books do you prefer reading?
    a. detective whodunnits
    b. historic romances

8. What would your ideal job be?
    a. a lawyer or a politician
    b. a nurse or a musician

9. How do you judge a person's character?
    a. by following your feelings
    b. by analysing the way they behave

10. What are you more likely to do if you know telling the truth will hurt someone's feelings?
    a. tell a white lie
    b. be brutally honest

ANSWERS

1. a-1 b-2	6. a-1 b-2
2. a-1 b-2	7. a-2 b-1
3. a-2 b-1	8. a-2 b-1
4. a-2 b-1	9. a-1 b-2
5. a-1 b-2	10. a-1 b-2

WHAT YOUR SCORE MEANS:

15-20 You're an analytical kind of person with strong principles and insist on being treated fairly. However, you have a tendency to hurt other people by being thoughtless and you should listen to your feelings more often.

10-14 You need praise and love. You're a good listener and like to please other people. But sometimes you're too passionate for your own good and act without thinking first. Try to introduce an element of balance into your decision-making.

FAITHFUL EVEN IN DEATH

The village of the Liang family and that of the Chu family were close together. The inhabitants were well-to-do and content. Old Excellency Liang and old Excellency Chu were good friends. A son was born to the Liang family, who was given the name Hsienpo. Being an unusually quick and clever child, he was sent to the school in the town.

At the same time a daughter was born to the Chu family, who, besides being very clever, was particularly beautiful. As a child she loved to read and study, and only needed to glance at a book to know a whole sentence by heart. Old Chu simply doted on her. When she grew up, she wanted to go away and study. Her father tried in vain to dissuade her, but eventually arranged for her to dress as a boy and study with Hsienpo.

The two lived together, worked together, argued together, and were the best of friends. The eager and zealous Hsienpo did not notice that Yingt'ai was really a girl, and therefore he did not fall in love with her. Yingt'ai studied so hard and was so wrapped up in her work that her fellow students paid no attention to her. Being very modest, and never taking part in the children's jokes, she exercised a calming influence over even the most impudent. When she slept with Hsienpo, each lay on one side of the bed, and between them stood a bowl of water. They had arranged that whoever knocked over the bowl must pay a fine; but the serious little Hsienpo never touched it.

When Yingt'ai changed her clothes, she never stood about naked but pulled on her clean clothes under the old ones, which she then took off and finished dressing. Her fellow students could not understand why she did this, and asked her the reason. "Only peasants expose the body they have received from their parents," she said; "it should not be done." Then the boys began to copy her, no knowing her real reason was to prevent their noticing that she was a girl.

Then her father died, and her sister-in-law, who did not approve of Yingt'ai's studying, ordered her to come home and learn housework. But Yingt'ai refused and continued to study.

The sister-in-law, fearing that Yingt'ai had fallen in love with Hsienpo, used to send her from time to time babies' things, swaddling clothes, children's clothes and covers, and many other things. The students became curious when they saw the things, and Yingt'ai could tell them only that they were the things she herself had used as a child, which her sister-in-law was now sending her to keep.

The time passed quickly. Soon Yingt'ai and Hsienpo were grown up. Yingt'ai still dressed as a man, and being a well-brought-up girl, she did not dare to ask Hsienpo to marry her; but when she looked at him her heart was filled with love. His delicate manner attracted her irresistibly, and she swore to marry him and none other.

She proposed the marriage to her sister-in-law, who did not consider it suitable, because after her father's death they had lost all their money. Against Yingt'ai's will the sister-in-law arranged a match with a Dr. Ma, of a newly rich family in the village. Yingt'ai objected strongly, but she could do nothing about it. Day after day she had to listen to complaints: she was without filial piety, she was a shameless, decadent girl, a disgrace to the family. Her sister-in-law still feared she might secretly marry Hsienpo, and she urged the Ma family to appoint a day for the wedding. Then she cut off Yingt'ai's school money, which forced her to return home.

Yingt'ai was obliged to hide her misery. Weeping bitterly, she said good-bye to Hsienpo, who accompanied her part of the way home. As they separated, Yingt'ai sang a song which revealed that she was a girl and that she wanted to marry him. But the good, dense Hsienpo did not understand her hints. He did not see into Yingt'ai's heart, and tried to comfort her by telling her that one must return home some time and that they would soon meet again. Yingt'ai saw that everything was hopeless and went home in tears.

Hsienpo felt very lonely without his companion, with whom he had lived day and night for many years. He kept on writing letters to Yingt'ai, begging her to come back to school, but he never received a reply.

Finally he could bear it no longer, and went to visit her. "Is Mr. Yingt'ai at home?" he asked. "Please tell him his school friend, Hsienpo, has come and wants to see him."

The servant looked at him curiously and then said curtly, "There is no Mr. Yingt'ai here - only a Miss Yingt'ai. She is to be married soon, and naturally she can't leave her room. How could she speak to a man? Please go away, sir, for if the master discovers you, he will make a complaint against you for improper behaviour."

Suddenly everything was clear to Hsienpo. In a state of collapse he crept home. There he found, under Yingt'ai's books, a bundle of letters and essays which showed him clearly how deeply Yingt'ai loved him and also that she did not want to marry any other man. Through his own stupidity, his lack of understanding, the dream had come to nought.

Overcome by remorse, he spent the days lost in tears. Yingt'ai was always before his eyes, and in his dreams he called her name, or cursed her sister-in-law and Dr. Ma, himself, and all the ways of society. Because he ceased to eat or drink, he fell ill and gradually sank into the grave.

Yingt'ai heard the sad news. Now she had nothing more to live for. If she had not been so carefully watched, she would have done herself some injury. In this state of despair the wedding day arrived. Listlessly she allowed herself to be pushed into the red bridal chair and set off for the house of her bridegroom, Dr. Ma. But when they passed the grave of Hsienpo, she begged her attendants to let her get out and visit it, to thank him for all his kindness. On the grave, overcome by grief, she flung herself down and sobbed. Her attendants urged her to return to her chair, but she refused. Finally, after great persuasion, she got up, dried her tears, and, bowing several times in front of the grave, she prayed as follows: "You are Hsienpo, and I am Yingt'ai. If we were really intended to be man and wife, open your grave three feet wide."

Scarcely had she spoken when there came a clap like thunder and the grave opened. Yingt'ai leaped into the opening, which closed again before the maids could catch hold of her, leaving only two bits of her dress in their hands. When they let these go, they changed into two butterflies which flew up into the air.

Dr. Ma was furious when he heard that his wife had jumped into the grave of Hsienpo. He had the grave opened, but the coffin was empty except for two white stones. No one knew where Hsienpo and Yingt'ai had gone. In a rage the grave violators flung the two stones onto the road, where immediately a bamboo with two stems shot up. They were shimmering green and swayed in the wind. The grave robbers knew that this was the result of magic, and cut down the bamboo with a knife; but as soon as they had cut down one, another shot up, until finally several people cut down the two stems at the same time. Then these flew up to heaven and became rainbows.

Now the two lovers have become immortals. If they ever want to be together, undisturbed and unseen, so that no one on earth can see them or even talk about them, they wait until it is raining and the clouds are hiding in the sky. The red in the rainbow is Hsienpo, and the blue is Yingt'ai.

(taken from *Best-Loved Folktales of The World* selected by Joanna Cole, Anchor Books 1982)

THE ENCHANTED WATER HOLE

Level: Upper Intermediate - Advanced
Target Audience: Secondary / Adults
Language / Skills Focus: Listening / Speaking / Writing
Materials: Photocopies of the worksheet. Photocopies of the story (optional) to hand out at the end of the session.

IN CLASS

1. *Pre-listening:* The story is about a magical water hole. What do you think will happen to anyone who drinks the water found there? Now listen to the story to find out whether your predictions were accurate or not.

2. *Post-Listening:* Hand out copies of the worksheet for the learners to work on in pairs.

   Match the numbers on the left with the letters on the right to find explanations for the new vocabulary: 1-m / 2-a / 3-o / 4-g / 5-j / 6-q / 7-d / 8-e / 9-l / 10-c / 11-I / 12-b / 13-h / 14-p / 15-f / 16-k / 17-n

   Pair-work Interviews. The learners ask each other the following questions, and then report back to the rest of the class with their findings:

   a. If you passed a wishing well, would you throw in a coin and make a wish or would you resist the temptation? Give the reasons for the choice you make.
   b. And if you made a wish, what would it be for and why?
   c. How superstitious are you?
   d. What examples of superstitions from your own country can you tell me about?
   e. How often do you read your horoscope and how seriously do you take it?
   f. Do you have a "lucky" number, charm, or colour? Tell me about it.
   g. What other stories do you know about people changing from human into animal form?

3. Brainstorm what other effects drinking enchanted water could have. Then invite the learners, working in small groups, to write parallel stories.

COMMENTS

This traditional tale from India can be used as a lead-in to the topic of *The Supernatural* and / or to facilitate parallel story writing.

THE ENCHANTED WATER HOLE

Once upon a time a couple lived happily in a village situated on a hill. Together they cleared the bushes and weeds from a patch of hillside. Then they planted their garden. In their labours the couple encountered many hardships, not least of which was lack of good streams or wells in the immediate area. Soon the wife was thirsty, and she pleaded with her husband to let her go in search of water. Although he loved her very much and sympathised with her, the husband would not let her go.

The husband knew of a water hole on the southern side of their property, but it was enchanted. "We cannot drink the water from the water hole to the south of our land," he told her. "Whoever drinks from this place will be turned into a tiger. No matter how thirsty you are, you must not drink that water," he said. His wife listened patiently as her husband talked, but still she pleaded with him to let her go looking for water. Finally he relented and allowed her to depart. He remained alone in the field. The wife searched and searched but nowhere could she find water, except in that forbidden water hole. Unable to bear her thirst any longer, she finally drank the enchanted water. After satisfying her thirst she returned to the field. She then lied to her husband, telling him that she had been careful not to drink from the forbidden pond but found water elsewhere.

The couple then went back to work together, but soon the wife began showing some tiger-like traits. When flies buzzed in front of her she caught them with her mouth! She also scratched at herself like a tiger! She still looked like a person, but from her behaviour her husband knew she must have drunk water from the enchanted pond. He was sad, for he knew that nothing could be done for her now. She, too, was sad. She loved and honoured her husband deeply, but she had lied to him. When evening came the two returned home. The wife now fed the children and put them to sleep. Then her husband ate and he, too, went to sleep. After everyone had bedded down, the woman left for the forest. She prowled here and there, just as a tiger might prowl in search of prey.

Although the water from the pond had affected her, this woman's love for her family was still strong. Each night she assumed the form of a tiger, but by day she was a wife and mother as usual. When she made a kill during the night she ate what she could and brought the remainder back for her family. One day she killed a man and brought the uneaten portion back to the house and left it on the verandah. Her husband was shocked. What could he do? Although his wife had drunk the water of the tiger pond and became a tiger at night, her love for him and their children kept her human during the day. He returned to the enchanted water hole and sealed it with a bison horn. Then he placed three big rocks around it so that no one else could drink water and turn into a tiger in this way.

THE ENCHANTED WATER HOLE: WORKSHEET

Match the numbers on the left with the letters on the right to find explanations for the new vocabulary:

1. bear
2. enchanted
3. encountered
4. hardships
5. in search of prey
6. labours
7. a patch
8. pleaded
9. pond
10. portion
11. prowl
12. relented
13. sympathised with
14. the remainder
15. traits
16. verandah
17. weeds

a. affected by magic
b. agreed to something previously refused
c. amount of food
d. an area of land
e. begged
f. characteristics
g. difficulties
h. felt sorry for
i. hunt
j. looking for animals to hunt
k. an extension to a house, but without an outside wall
l. a small area of water
m. tolerate / put up with
n. unwanted wild plants
o. were obliged to face
p. what was left of
q. work

Working in pairs, ask each other the following questions, then report back to the rest of the class with your findings:

a. If you passed a wishing well, would you throw in a coin and make a wish or would you resist the temptation? Give the reasons for the choice you make.
b. And if you made a wish, what would it be for and why?
c. How superstitious are you?
d. What examples of superstitions from your own country can you tell me about?
e. How often do you read your horoscope and how seriously do you take it?
f. Do you have a "lucky" number, charm, or colour? Tell me about it.
g. What other stories do you know about people changing from human into animal form?

TOM COCKLE

Level: Intermediate - Advanced
Target Audience: Adults
Language / Skills Focus: Listening, Speaking & Writing
Materials: Photocopies of the worksheet. Photocopies of the story (optional) to hand out at the end of the session.

NOTES FOR TEACHERS

1. *Pre-listening:* When you're based in a foreign country and feel homesick, who and / or what do you miss most, and why? Turn to the person sitting to your left, and tell them about it.

2. Do you have someone or something that you feel brings you good luck, or perhaps a good luck charm you always keep with you? Turn to the person sitting next to your right and tell them about it.

3. The story you are about to hear is an Irish version of a Tom Cockle tale that deals with the problem of homesickness. Tom Cockle is a hob – a friendly and helpful spirit who can help people through such difficulties

4. *Post-listening:* Read through the story to find words which mean the same as the following: a. They were homesick for their old home / b. fell on bad times / c. they had to leave Ireland for good / d. tried to cheer them up all the way / e. there was always something to hand

5. Match the numbers on the left with the letters on the right to find explanations for the new vocabulary: 1-i / 2-g / 3-b / 4-k / 5-h / 6-f / 7-c / 8-d / 9-e / 10-a / 11-j

6. Invite the learners to write parallel stories of their own about homesickness and the following questions can be used facilitate the process.

    a. Who do you feel looked over you or protected you when you were in your country?
    b. What did you use to come home to in the evenings after work / school?
    c. What do you come home to after work / school now that you're here?
    d. Who can be here to look over you now that you're here and what conditions can they create to make you feel more at home?

7. The students can then tell each other their stories in small groups or circles. Make a note of effective language used and any errors that crop up which can be dealt with at the end of the session.

COMMENTS

The story is an Irish version of a *Tom Cockle* tale that deals with homesickness, something all foreign students experience at one time or another. It is hoped that the telling of the tale and the activities that follow it will have a cathartic effect.

TOM COCKLE

There was a family who come from the mountains of Ireland to live in the English Lake District, and they didn't want to come but they had to. They were homesick for their old home and they hated leaving their luck behind.

His name was Tom Cockle and he had taken care of them for hundreds of years. No one ever saw him but the countryside knew he was there. Somehow there was always a meal and a bed however many might turn up even when the family fell on bad times.

At last the times were so bad and dangerous they had to leave Ireland for good and go to the mother's English home in the North Country, but before they went they had to tell Tom Cockle they were going.

The father and mother called out and told him. "Oh, Tom, dear Tom Cockle, it's having to leave Ireland and you we are, and our hearts are broken on us." Then they went away and they all cried at the going.

The mother tried to cheer them up all the way, but there was muddle and hunger and loss every minute by land and sea.

"At least we'll be away from the cities and in mountains," the children comforted each other. "And fell ponies to ride, and trout in the streams and wild fowl in the lakes," but the mother wondered to herself how she's manage the old, cold, empty house. She had loved it, but it needed twenty servants or a Tom Cockle to light fires, and fill larders, and sweep, and cook, and warm their hearts, and Tom Cockle was away back in Ireland. And in Ireland she only had to call out to Tom and tell him what she needed and there was always something to hand.

She bravely hid her tears, and as they drove the pony through the rain to her new, old home she made plans for a fire and at least a drop of porridge. It was bad enough coming over dark mountains on a cold, rainy night to an empty house. They had always come home to a welcome in Ireland. Tom Cockle had seen to that.

Then one of the children cried out, "There's the house down there, it's got lights!" Yes, it was their new, empty house, but there was a fire in the hearth, food on the table, fodder in the stable and lights to welcome them – Tom Cockle had got there before them.

TOM COCKLE: WORKSHEET

Read through the story to find words which mean the same as the following:

a. They missed the place where they had lived before
b. experienced hardship
c. they were forced to emigrate
d. attempted to raise their spirits on the journey
e. he always provided them with what they required

Match the numbers on the left with the letters on the right to find explanations for the new vocabulary:

1.	cheer them up	a. arrive
2.	fodder	b. a bird kept for its meat and eggs
3.	fowl	c. a breakfast cereal made of oats and water or milk
4.	hearth	d. a building to keep horses in
5.	larders	e. a type of river fish
6.	muddle	f. confusion
7.	porridge	g. food for animals kept on farms
8.	stable	h. large cupboards you can walk into for food
9.	trout	i. make them feel happier
10.	turn up	j. missed
11.	were homesick for	k. the floor around a fireplace

Write a parallel story of your own about homesickness. Your answers to the following questions might give you some ideas:

a. Who do you feel looked over you or protected you when you were in your country?
b. What did you use to come home to in the evenings after work / school?
c. What do you come home to after work / school now that you're here?
d. Who can be here to look over you now that you're here and what conditions can they create to make you feel more at home?

HOW THE GYPSY WENT TO HEAVEN

Level: Upper Intermediate - Advanced

Target Audience: Adults

Language / Skills Focus: Listening & Speaking

IN CLASS

1 *Pre-listening*: Ask the learners, working individually, to make a list of the four things they want most in life, then to compare them with what the man in the story chose!

2 An alternative lead-in to the tale could be the following: *How can an apple tree, a blanket, an iron box and a turban help you get to heaven when you die?*

   The learners could be invited to discuss this in groups, then report back to the class with their findings.

3 *Post-listening*: Ask the learners to pair up and compare the choices they made at the start. And, with the benefit of hindsight, they might now wish to re-assess their priorities.

THE STORY

Once God visited a small Gypsy village, and nobody was there except the blacksmith and his wife. And so God slept all night at their house. When morning came, the blacksmith's wife said to God, "I want to go to heaven when I die.

And God said to her, "You're such a good wife that you can't end up in hell. There's all that crying and suffering there. And as for your husband, because I had such a nice, peaceful night, I'm going to give him the four things that he wants most in his life." So God asked him what he wanted most in his life.

The blacksmith answered, "The first thing I want is this: whatever man I tell to go up in my apple tree, may he never come down until I say so. This is the first thing I want. And whoever I tell to go sit on my horse's blanket, may they never get up again unless I tell them to. These are the two things that I want most in my life."

"And the third thing?" asked God.

"Whoever goes into my little iron box, may they never come out till I say so."

And God said, "Okay, that's three things. And the last thing?"

"I want my turban with me all my life, and when I sit on it, may no man be able to make me get up."

Well the Gypsy blacksmith lived a very long time. But one day after many years the angel of death came to him and said, "Come with me."

And the Gypsy said, "Just let me say goodbye to my wife and my family first."

The angel said, "Okay."

And the Gypsy told him. "Why don't you go up in my apple tree and wait there for me. I'll be right along."

So the angel of death climbed up the apple tree as the Gypsy suggested but he couldn't come down again. Then the Gypsy said to him, "You let me live another twenty years and then I'll let you come down."

And the angel of death said, "Okay, you'll live another twenty years."

After another twenty years the angel of death came a second time and said to the Gypsy, "Your time is up. You must come with me."

This time the Gypsy said, "Just let me say goodbye to my children and make things ready for them. You go and sit on my horse's blanket."

The angel of death went to sit on the horse's blanket and he found that he couldn't get up.

"What's this?" he said. "I can't get up again."

And the Gypsy said, "Give me another twenty years to live and then I'll let you get up."

"Okay, Okay, you can live another twenty years." The angel of death had no choice.

After another twenty years the Devil came to the Gypsy and said, "Now is your time. You come with me."

"You're so clever," the Gypsy said to the Devil. Then he added, "Let me see you get into that little iron box, if you can."

The Devil said, "I can get in there - no problem."

The iron box became red-hot and the Devil tried to get out of it. But the Gypsy placed it in the fire.

The Devil fought and fought to escape until he had no strength left. And the Gypsy said, "If I let you get out of the box, you have to leave me alone forever."

And the Devil said, "Okay. You win. I don't want to see you ever again."

Another twenty years passed, and another angel of death came - the one who judges where you should go - and said to the Gypsy, "Your time has come."

The Gypsy said, "First I have some work to do in my house."

"Your time has come," said the angel. "And this time you can't say no."

So he took him first to the Devil. And the Devil said, "No, I don't want him here. Get him out of here, quick!"

And then the angel took the Gypsy to God, who said, "No, I don't want him here either. Please take him away."

And the Gypsy said to God, "Can I just see what your kingdom is like before I go?"

The Gypsy opened the door a bit and looked through the crack. Then he threw his turban in, sat down on it and nobody could get him off it again. And that's how the Gypsy went to heaven.

THE PROPHECY

Level: Upper Intermediate / Advanced
Target Audience: Secondary, Adults
Language / Skills Focus: Listening & Speaking
Materials: Enough blanks cards or slips of paper for everyone in the group

IN CLASS

1 *Pre-listening*: You could start with a brainstorming session to find out how much the class already know about prophets and their prophecies. Alternatively you could name some prophets, Isaiah, Mohammed, and Nostradamus, and ask the class what they all had in common.

2 *While-listening*: Stop after reading the first paragraph and ask the learners to predict what the prophecy was.

3 Stop after "clouds spread across the sky and the thunder and the lightning began" and the students to predict what happened next.

4 *Post-listening*: Hand out a blank card / slip of paper to everyone in the group and ask them to write their names on them. Collect the cards in and redistribute them, making sure that nobody gets their own name. Ask each person to write a prophecy about the person whose name card they have, starting with the words *Ten years from now this person will* ..... Invite the learners to read out their prophecies and for the rest of the class to guess the identity of the person being referred to. This activity requires little preparation and can be used to provide controlled practice in talking about the future.

5 The king's son had a choice between accepting the prophecy or of attempting to create his own fate. What course of action would you have taken in his place? How do you feel about astrology and other methods of predicting the future? Have you ever been to a fortune-teller and did the predictions that were made come true? These questions could be discussed in groups, with a spokesperson chosen in each group to present their findings to the class as a whole.

COMMENTS

At the end of the session you might like to distribute photocopies of the tale. You could invite the learners to highlight all the language they do understand rather than underline the words that they do not. This approach helps to boost the learners' self-confidence by showing them how much they already know instead of focusing on what they do not know.

THE PROPHECY

Long ago there was a king who was very rich and powerful. The only thing that troubled him and his wife, the queen, was that they had no children. Well, at long last there was a child coming, and the king got very excited about it. He had priests and bishops and wise men and doctors and nurses all ready for the special occasion. And just before the child was born, it was in the middle of the night, he brought all the wise men up to the castle, to tell him about the child's future. And there was one of the wise men who could read the stars and make prophecies from them, and this is what he said.

'The child will be a boy,' said the wise man, 'and he will grow up strong, handsome and clever. And there is no son of a king in the whole world that will be his equal,' the wise man added, reading the stars all the time. 'But what's this I see? It's written in the stars that when the son of the king is twenty-one years of age, he's to be killed by a flash of lightning.' And the wise man wrote down the message on paper and handed it to the king, that twenty-one years exactly from the day he was born, the son of the king would be hit by lightning and killed.

The child was born the same night, a fine baby boy. And he grew up just as the wise man prophesied; there was not a king's son in the world that was his equal in good looks, in learning, in strength or in courage, and the people of the kingdom would do anything for him. And the old king never told a single person about the prophecy, and he warned the wise man to say nothing about it either, or it would be the worse for him. Although he was greatly frightened and troubled, he did not want to be putting trouble and sorrow on his son and on the queen and on all the people, and that is why he kept it to himself.

But when the son of the king was about nineteen years old, he noticed his father directing a team of workmen who were putting up a great big fortification of some sort on the side of a hill about a mile away from the castle. And when he asked his father what the building was for, the king refused to tell him. As for the workmen, they knew little either, only that they were to build a wall here and a door there and a window somewhere else according to the king's instructions, until the building was all finished. Finally, the day before his twenty-first birthday, the old king took his son to one side, showed him the paper and told him about the prophecy.

'And now,' said the king, 'I'm going to put you into the fort, and you're to stay there until all the thunder and lightning is over. And you can be sure that no lightning will touch you there as it will protect you from the danger.'

So the king's son went into the fort and sat down. Although there was plenty to eat and drink there, he was in no mood for eating and drinking. He was greatly troubled by what the king told him. And he was thinking to himself that if it was the will of God that he would be killed, all the stone and mortar in the world would not save him. And finally he got so troubled that he could not stand being inside in the fort any more, so he searched around until he found an open window, for the old king had the doors locked and barred. He crept out through the window, and away down to the river and threw himself down on the mossy bank. It was a fine hot day in the beginning of August, and he was soon fast asleep.

And while he was asleep, dark clouds spread across the sky and the thunder and lightning began. There came a most frightful flash that lit up the whole sky, followed by a deafening rumble, and the lightning hit the fort and made dust of it. And the king, the royal household, and all the people came running out in the rain, in dread the king's son was killed. But the next thing was that they saw him coming up from the river, and all the danger passed, and the mourning soon turned to rejoicing.

As for the king, he lived on until a ripe old age, and when his time eventually came to an end, his son took over and ruled the kingdom in his place.

(adapted from a story in "Folktales From The Irish Countryside" by Kevin Danaher, Mercier Press 1998)

THE CLEVER THIEF

Level: Upper Intermediate / Advanced
Target Audience: Secondary / Adults
Language / Skills Focus: Listening, Speaking & Writing / Money Idioms
Materials: Photocopies of the worksheets (the story and the matching activity)

IN CLASS

1   The following questions can be used to lead into the topic: Have you ever stolen anything? Tell me about it. Can theft ever be justified and if it can be justified, in what circumstances?

2   Imagine you were arrested for stealing something and sent to prison. How many different ways of escaping can you come up with? Invite the students to work in small groups and to list all the ways they can think of - digging a tunnel, kidnapping one of the guards, or jumping over the wall, for example. Invite a spokesperson from each group to read out their suggestions. Well, you've come up with a lot of inventive ideas but nobody has found the way the thief used in the story that follows!

3   As a post-listening activity, the students can work on the "Money Idioms" activity in pairs. Invite the first pair to finish to board their answers – the numbers and the letters - and the rest of the class to say whether they agree or not.

Match the idioms on the left with the explanations on the right. There are more explanations than you need so make sure you select the correct ones! 1-l / 2-k / 3-i / 4-f / 5-h / 6-n / 7-j / 8-g / 9-m / 10-c

4   You can then arrange the learners in groups of four to write a short story or a dialogue incorporating as many of the idioms as they can. The group who include the most idioms can be given a prize. Alternatively, the students could take it in turns to mime one of the idioms for the others to guess. This can be hilarious and makes the language impossible to forget!

5   There are lots of stories in the news about corrupt politicians and officials. Can you think of any recent examples? What do you think the cause of corruption is and what can be done to prevent it?

6   The following task could be set for homework: Write a letter to "The Clever Thief" asking for advice or write a letter from "The Clever Thief" to you giving advice.

THE CLEVER THIEF

In Korea, many years ago, there once lived an old thief who as known throughout the country as a very clever person - far too clever to be captured. However, one morning he was so careless and overconfident that he was caught stealing some spices from a shopkeeper. With great satisfaction the police brought the thief before an extremely severe judge who fined the old man very heavily. Unable to pay the sum, the thief had to submit instead to a very lengthy jail sentence. When he arrived at the prison he examined with great thoroughness his cell and the building itself, looking for a means of escape. Finding none, he soon gave up the idea of escape and instead decided upon another way of getting out of jail. Early one morning he called for the jail keeper.

"Yes," the keeper inquired gruffly, "what do you want?"

"Take me before the king," demanded the thief.

"The king!" The jail keeper threw back his head and gasped with laughter. "Why should the king see you?"

The thief ignored the jail keeper's scorn.

"Tell him I have a gift for him - of extraordinary value."

The jail keeper, impressed with the old man's seriousness, finally agreed to arrange the interview.

The next afternoon the thief was taken to the royal quarters. There the king sat upon an enormous throne, looking very impressive and stern.

"Well, what is it? What do you have for me?" asked the king. "I don't have all day to spend on the likes of you, you know."

Before replying, the thief noted that the prime minister, the secretary of state, the head of the army, and the head jail keeper were also present.

"Your Majesty," said the thief, "I have come here to present you with a rare and valuable gift." Slipping his hand into his pocket, he carefully withdrew a tiny box, elegantly wrapped in gold paper with silver ribbons.

The king took the package and swiftly opened it. Examining the contents, his face suddenly flushed red with rage and his voice filled the room with a series of royal bellows.

"What is the meaning of this? How dare you bring me an ordinary plum pit!"

"True," admitted the old thief quietly, "it is a plum pit." Here he paused for emphasis. "But by no means an ordinary one."

"What do you mean by that?" stormed the king.

"He who plants this pit," stated the old man, "will reap nothing but golden plums."

A moment of astonished silence greeted this news.

Finally the king said, "Well, if that's the case, why haven't you planted it yourself?"

"For a very good reason, Your Majesty," answered the thief. "Only people who have never stolen or cheated can reap the benefit. Otherwise, the tree will bear only ordinary plums. That is why," and the old thief smiled in his most winning way, "I have brought the pit to you. Certainly, Your Majesty has never stolen anything or cheated."

"Alas," declared the king with great regret in his voice - for he was an honest man no matter what other faults he had - "I'm afraid I am not the right person."

"What do you mean?" cried the others present.

But the king remained silent, remembering how he had once stolen some pennies from his mother's purse when he was a little boy.

"Well, how about the prime minister?" suggested the thief. "Perhaps he - "But the old thief got no further with his sentence.

"Impossible!" blustered the prime minister with a very red face. He had often accepted bribes from people who wanted fine positions in the government. Surely, the pit would never work for him.

"You then, General?" asked the thief, turning to the head of the army.

"No, no," muttered the general with lowered eyes. He had become an enormously rich man by cheating his soldiers of part of their pay.

"Well then, Mr. Secretary of State?" offered the thief.

"I'm afraid not," sputtered the honourable old man, whose conscience was obviously troubling him. Like the prime minister, he had at times accepted money in return for favours.

"Then the head jail keeper must be our man," said the thief solemnly as he turned to the last candidate.

Silently the jail keeper shook his head and shrugged his shoulders.

"I'm afraid I'm not right either," he said at last. He was remembering how he was always treating new prisoners, sending those who gave him money to the best quarters and reserving the worst cells for the poor and unfortunate.

Refusing to give up, the thief suggested several other officials. Each of the fine gentlemen, however, rejected in his turn the offer of the plum pit that would bear him golden fruit forever. When the room was entirely still, each official trying to hide his embarrassment, the old thief suddenly burst out laughing.

"You gentlemen," he exclaimed, "you embezzle and you steal, and yet you never end up in jail!"

He searched their faces earnestly, and then in a quiet voice, he added, "I have done nothing more than steal some spices, and for this I have been condemned to serve five years in jail." For quite some time the king and his officials remained silent with shame.

At last the king stirred.

"I would suggest," he said in a low voice, looking at each of his ministers one by one, "that we all contribute to this man's fine, so that he will not go back to jail."

Immediately the necessary money was gathered and placed at the monarch's feet. Calling the old thief to him, the king gave him the money.

"Go, my good man," he said. "You are free. You have spent enough time in prison. From your experience you have instructed us wisely. Ministers and kings sometimes forget themselves. We will remember your lesson well."

And so, with nothing more than a plum pit to help him, the very clever old thief left jail a free man.

MONEY IDIOMS Match the idioms on the left with the explanations on the right. There are more explanations than you need so make sure you select the correct ones!

1. You must be made of money.
2. It's money for old rope.
3. Money is clearly no object for you.
4. Money is the root of all evil.
5. Money talks.
6. Put your money where your mouth is.
7. You spend money like it's going out of fashion.
8. Money doesn't grow on trees.
9. You gave me a good run for my money.
10. Don't throw good money after bad.

a. Gambling is a risky business.
b. Having money turns people into criminals.
c. I advise you to cut your losses.
d. I'm not as fast as you.
e. It's money foolishly spent.
f. The main cause of crime is greed.
g. The supply of money isn't limitless.

h. Wealth can be used to influence people.
i. You're lucky because you don't have to worry.
j. You're rather wasteful of money, aren't you?
k. You get paid well for little effort.
l. You must be very wealthy.
m. You proved to be a worthy opponent.
n. You should back your beliefs with action.

THE PROPHECIES OF OLD MOTHER SHIPTON

Level: Upper Intermediate / Advanced
Target Audience: Secondary, Adults
Language / Skills Focus: Listening & Speaking / Talking about the future
Materials: Photocopies of the worksheet. Photocopies of the story (optional) to hand out to the learners after the session.

IN CLASS

1   *Pre-listening:* Start with a brainstorming session, to find out what the class already knows about witches. You can pin up a picture of a witch in the centre of the board to start the process off, then invite the learners up to the front to board the ideas they come up. An alternative would be to find out how much they know about Nostradamus, then to introduce Mother Shipton as the English equivalent.

2   *While-listening:* Pause after "what does that prove?" and ask the learners to predict what follows - why she threw her shawl in the fire. You can also pause after "the only way to rid the country of such evil practices" and ask the learners to predict the ending of the tale - and what do you think happened next?

3   *Post-listening:* Match the numbers on the left with the letters on the right to find explanations for the new language 1-f / 2-k / 3-g / 4-l / 5-m / 6-b / 7-d / 8-a / 9-e / 10-c / 11-n / 12-j / 13-h / 14-i

4   This can be followed by the groupwork activity, which involves the interpretation of Mother Shipton's predictions and the formulation of additional prophecies about the future. This can provide an opportunity to practise the different future forms and for expressing degrees of certainty.

5   To conclude the session, the script for a guided visualisation is provided. It is recommended that it should be read to a musical accompaniment to help create a suitable atmosphere. The class can then be split into two circles in which the learners can discuss their journeys and the insights they had in the process.

A GUIDED VISUALISATION: TO OLD MOTHER SHIPTON

SCRIPT FOR THE GUIDE: (to be read in a gentle trance-inducing voice) Make yourself comfortable and close your eyes. Take a few deep breaths to help your relax. Feel the tension disappear stage by stage from the top of your head to the tips of your toes. Let your surroundings fade away as you gradually sink backwards through time and actuality and pass through the gateway of reality into the dreamtime. (When the participants are fully relaxed, begin the next stage)

You're walking along a path overgrown with weeds, under a canopy of trees, with the light of the full moon to guide you. Feel the greenery brush against you, smell the scent of pine in the breeze, and hear the sounds of nature all around you. Now you find yourself facing the mouth of a cave. The opening is low and you have to stoop down to enter. At first you find it difficult to see anything but gradually you become accustomed to the darkness. You feel your way through the descending tunnel by placing your hands on the walls and it eventually widens out into circular cavern.

There you find Mother Shipton seated by a fire, her face illuminated by the flickering flames. You know there were many in her lifetime that were frightened of her. But you also know that despite her reputation, she only harmed those who intended to harm her and that you have nothing to fear from her. Take a minute of clock time, equal to all the time you need, to introduce yourself to the wise old soul, and to tap into the source of her wisdom .....

Perhaps you're at a crossroad in your life and don't know which direction to take. Or perhaps you have a question on your mind that's been troubling you and you feel you need some guidance. Only you know what you're looking for, only you know the question that's right for you to ask at this time in you life. And you have a minute of clock time, equal to all the time you need to ask her your question and listen to her answer .....

You look around you to find a gift to leave Mother Shipton, to thank her for the help she has given you, something found in nature - perhaps a feather, a flower or a stone. How misunderstood this poor woman was during her lifetime on earth and you're grateful to have the opportunity to show her your appreciation and to help redress the balance. You have a minute of clock time, equal to all the time you need, to find something appropriate ......

And now the time has come for you to make your way home, but not empty-handed. Because you're returning with the knowledge to help you face the next stage of your journey through life and you feel thankful for the insights you've been given. And so you return, back along the overgrown path, but with a feeling of lightness, as if a great weight has been removed from your shoulders. Back you walk, under the canopy of trees, listening to the sounds of nature and sensing the Great Mystery all around you - the Great Mystery that you're very much part of, back, back, the same way you came, and back to the place you started from. Welcome Home!

Take a deep breath, hold it, let it all out, open your eyes and smile at the first person you see.

Take a few minutes in silence to make some notes on the experiences you had on your journey, which you can then share with the rest of the group.

THE PROPHECIES OF OLD MOTHER SHIPTON: WORKSHEET

Match the numbers on the left with the letters on the right to find explanations for the new language:

1.	prophecies	a. amazement
2.	they disguised themselves	b. getting angry
3.	set off	c. in a threatening way
4.	astounded	d. laughed in a horrible way
5.	with a reputation for	e. more evidence
6.	losing his temper	f. predictions about the future
7.	cackled	g. started a journey
8.	astonishment	h. the crime of betraying your country by helping its enemies
9.	further proof	i. the king or queen
10.	menacingly	j. the sound of horses' feet on stones
11.	evil practices	k. they changed the way they looked
12.	the clatter of hooves	l. very surprised
13.	treason	m. well known for
14.	the monarch	n. wicked behaviour

Mother Shipton was famous for her prophecies, like Nostradamus. Working in small groups, read through the following prediction she made. Which of them can you identify? Then make some prophecies for the future of your own!

Carriages without horses will go
And accidents fill the world with woe.
Iron on the water will float
As easy as a wooden boat.
Under the water men will walk,
Will ride, will sleep, will eat, will talk.
Up in the air men will be seen
In white, in black, in red, in green.
A house of glass will come to pass
In England here, but will not last.
War will follow the construction work
In lands of the Pagan, and the Turk.
Around the world men's thoughts will fly
All in the twinkling of an eye.
Gold will be found again, and found
In a land that is not yet known.
- Mother Shipton

THE PROPHECIES OF OLD MOTHER SHIPTON

When Mother Shipton heard the news that the great Cardinal Wolsey, second in importance only to the king himself, was going to visit York, this is what she said:

"He may plan to do so, but set foot in York he never will."

Word of mouth quickly carried her prophecy about the visit to the great man's ears. He was not surprisingly angry and sent three of his noblemen to question her - the Duke of Suffolk, Lord Percy and Lord Darcy. When they reached York, they called on a gentleman called Besley, who agreed to take them to see her. They disguised themselves so they would not be recognized, then set off for her house. Led by Besley, they approached her door and knocked. A voice from the inside called out at once:

"Come in Master Besley and let the noble lords follow. You know the way, and they don't."

Astounded by her foreknowledge of who her visitors were, they nervously entered. Mother Shipton was sitting by the fire. She welcomed each of them by name, in spite of their disguise, and provided them with refreshments as if she were a great lady, instead of a simple country person with a reputation for being a witch.

The noble Duke of Suffolk was embarrassed by her kindness.

"My good woman," said the Duke, "when you know what we have come for, you will probably not be so pleased to see us. You have prophesied that Cardinal Wolsey will never see York!"

"No, I didn't. What I said was that he might see York but he would never set foot in the city!"

"It's the same thing," said the Duke, losing his temper. Prophecy is an evil thing and when the Cardinal does come, you will be burned at the stake as a witch."

"Will I indeed?" she cackled, and to their astonishment she took off the shawl that covered her shoulders and threw it into the fireplace. Although the flames rose and licked all around it, miraculously it did not burn. After a few minutes, she lifted it out of the fire, replacing it round her shoulders just as before.

"What did you do that for?" asked the startled Duke. "What does that prove?"

"Don't you understand? If my shawl had burned in the fire, then I might have burned at the stake. But as the one did not burn, neither will the other!"

"Don't be so sure," said the angry Duke menacingly, and without waiting for further proof of her powers, he made off, followed by the others.

Soon afterwards, Cardinal Wolsey set out for York, and stayed overnight at the village of Cawood, about eight miles outside the city.

"I'm on my way to York," he told his hosts, "but some crazy old woman has said that I will never see it."

"No, my Lord," his host said. "Her words were that you would see it, but never set foot inside its walls. In fact, you can see it from here. Look, there are its walls clearly to be seen."

Then the great man looked, and sure enough, the walls of York eight miles away were caught by the evening sunlight, and showed up clearly against the surrounding hills."

"Tomorrow I will arrive in York," said His Eminence. "And as soon as I am within the gates of the city, this woman will be burned at the stake - the only way to rid the country of such evil practices."

Just then, the clatter of hooves was heard on the cobbled courtyard, and looking down, the Cardinal saw King Henry VIII's men. They had come with orders to arrest him and take him back to London to answer charges of treason brought by the monarch against him.

So he never did set foot in York, and he never even saw London again. Worn out with ill-health and sorrow, he died in Leicester soon after. And Mother Shipton had proved a true prophetess once again.

TAHOTAHONTANEKENTSERATKERONTAKWENHAKIE

Level: Intermediate - Advanced
Target Audience: Secondary / Adults
Language / Skills Focus: Listening, Speaking & Writing
Materials: Photocopies of the worksheet, enough copies for one between two. Photocopies of the story (optional) to hand out at the end of the session.

IN CLASS

1   The pre-listening tasks can be found on the worksheet. The learners can work on these in pairs or small groups. There is also a post-listening activity on the sheet, which leads into providing practice in giving definitions. The names of the professions that the people practise are a busker/ a plumber / acrobats / an acupuncturist / an undertaker

2   As a post-listening activity, you can ask the learners to work in small groups to write a story about someone with an unusual name, explaining how he or she got it. It could be a true story or an imaginary one.

3   Elicit or explain what a tongue twister is (a word or a phrase that is difficult to say quickly or correctly - like the title of this story) Ask the class if they know any other examples and then invite them to practise the following or any other that you know: *Betty Boater bought some butter but she said this butter's bitter and a bit of better butter will make my batter better so she bought a bit of butter better than the bitter butter and it was better Betty Boater bought a bit of better butter!*

COMMENTS

This Native American tale was written by Salli Benedict and is taken from the collection *Earth Power Coming,* published by Navajo Community College Press 1983. Written permission to use this story was sought but no reply was received from the publisher.

TAHOTAHONTANEKENTSERATKERONTAKWENHAKIE: WORKSHEET

Here are some English names. Which ones do you like, which names have equivalents in your own language, and which one would you like to choose for yourself?

BOYS NAMES: Adam, Brian, Charles, David, Edward, Frank, George, Harry, John, Kevin, Laurence, Michael, Neil, Oliver, Peter, Rodney, Stewart, Thomas, Vincent, William

GIRLS NAMES: Angela, Bridget, Christine, Diana, Emily, Fiona, Gina, Hannah, Ingrid, Jacqueline, Kim, Louise, Mandy, Nicola, Paula, Ruth, Sharon, Tracey, Victoria, Wendy

How do you address the following people in your country - by their first names or their family names?

a. your teacher   b. your boss   c. your colleagues

Work in pairs. Take it in turns to ask each other the following questions:

a. What do you know about the origin of your own name?
b. Have you got a nickname? If so, what is it and how did you get it?
c. Have you ever had any interesting experiences because of your name?
d. If you had children of your own, what would you name them and why?
e. If you had children of your own, would you like them to call you mummy or daddy or to call you by your first name?

In the story, the old man who gave the boy his name was a seller of rabbits. Now see if you can name the professions that the following people practise:

a. This person plays music on street corners and in underground stations and people passing by give him / her money.
b. This person clears sinks and drains when they get blocked and can also see to leaking pipes.
c. These people work in a circus and can stand on their heads and do somersaults.
d. This person is a practitioner of alternative medicine who sticks needles in people to help them get better.
e. When someone dies, this person sees to the funeral arrangements and the burial of the body.

Now prepare five questions of your own like the examples above to test the person sitting next to you with:

TAHOTAHONTANEKENTSERATKERONTAKWENHAKIE

Deep in the woods, there lived a man and his wife, and their newborn baby boy. The baby was so young that his parents had not yet given him a name. Hunting was very bad that winter and they had very little to eat. They were very poor.

One day around suppertime, a little old man came to their door. He was selling rabbits.

"Do you wish to buy a rabbit for your supper?" he asked.

The woman who met him at the door replied that they were very poor and had no money to buy anything.

It was growing dark and the man looked very tired. The woman knew that he had travelled very far just to see if they would buy a rabbit from him. She invited him to stay for supper and share what little they had to eat.

"What is your name?" the husband asked as he got up to meet the old man.

"I have no name," the little man replied. "My parents were lost before they could name me. People just call me Tahotahontanekentseratkerontakwenhakie which means, 'He came and sold rabbits.' "

The husband laughed. "My son has not been named yet either. We just call him The Baby."

The old man said, "You should name him so that he will know who he is. There is great importance in a name." The old man continued, "I will give you this last rabbit of mine for a good supper, so that we may feast in honour of the birth of your new son."

In the morning, the old man left. The parents of the baby still pondered over a name for the baby.

"We shall name the baby after the generous old man who gave him a feast in honour of his birth. But he has no name," the mother said.

"Still, we must honour his gift to our son," the husband replied. "We will name our son after what people call the old man, Tahotahontanekentseratkerontakwenhakie which means, 'He came and sold rabbits.'"

"What a long name that is," the mother said. "Still, we must honour the old man's wish for a name for our son and his feast for our son."

So the baby's name became Tahotahontanekentseratkerontakwenhakie which means, "He came and sold rabbits," in honour of the old man.

The baby boy grew older and became very smart, He had to be, to be able to remember his own name. Like all other children he was always trying to avoid work. He discovered that by the time his mother had finished calling his name for chores, he could be far, far away.

Sometimes his mother would begin telling him some thing to do, "Tahotahontanekentseratkerontakwenhakie . . . hmmmm . . ." She would forget what she wanted to have him do, so she would smile and tell him to go and play.

Having such a long important name had its disadvantages too. When his family travelled to other settlements to visit friends and other children, the other children would leave him out of games. They would not call him to play or catch ball. They said that it took more energy to say his name than it did to play the games.

News of this long, strange name travelled to the ears of the old man,

Tahotahontanekentserakerontakwenhakie. "What a burden this name must be for a child," the old man thought. "This name came in gratitude for my feast for the birth of the boy. I must return to visit them."

The old man travelled far to the family of his namesake, Tahotahontanekentseratkerontakwenhakie. The parents met the old man at the door and invited him in. He brought with him food for another fine meal.

"You are very gracious to honour me with this namesake," he said. "But we should not have two people wandering this world, at the same time, with the same name. People will get us confused, and it may spoil my business. Let us call your son Oiasosonaion which means, 'He has another name.' If people wish to know his other name, then he can tell them."

Oiasosonaion smiled and said, "I will now have to call you Tahotahontanekentseratkerontakwenhakie tanon Oiasahosonnon which means, 'He came and sold rabbits and gave the boy another name.'"

Everyone laughed.

CRAB

Level: Upper Intermediate / Advanced

Target Audience: Secondary, Adults

Language / Skills Focus: Listening & Speaking

Materials: Photocopies of the worksheet. Photocopies of the story (optional) to hand out to the learners after the session.

IN CLASS

1   *Pre-listening:* The Pair-work Interviews on the worksheet can be used to provide a lead-in to the topic. Ask the learners to work in pairs and invite them to take it in turns to ask each other the questions. They then report back to the rest of the class with their findings. With larger classes, to speed up the process, two circles can be formed for the feedback stage. The story is about how a king's willingness to believe in the powers of astrology led to his being taken advantage of and it comes from Italy.

2   *Post-listening:* Return to the worksheet for the second activity, which the students can work on individually. They can then pair up to compare their answers to see if they agree with each other.

Read through the story to find words which mean the same as the following: a. he issued a proclamation / b. but took it into his head / c. That is at your discretion / d. from the severe glances that the peasant cast at them / e. they began to fear that they would be found out / f. never opened their mouths without calling him / g. denounces us to the king as thieves / h. we are lost / i. ask him not to betray us / j. what a plight you are in!"

3   *We learn from the story that Crab could neither read nor write. What other situations can you think of in which being illiterate could be an advantage? Make a list of them.*

Invite the learners to work in pairs or small groups on this, and the pair or group that produces the longest list could be awarded a prize (You can save free soaps, shampoos, bubble baths, and shower caps from hotels where you stay to use for this purpose. Alternatively, if you're feeling particularly cruel, the prize could be extra homework!).

4   Now match the numbers with the letters to complete these proverbs about crime and punishment: 1-b / 2-g / 3-f / 4-a / 5-j / 6-c / 7-h / 8-i / 9-d / 10-e

After the matching activity, the students can be invited to work in pairs to write dialogues incorporating as many of the proverbs as they can. These can then be read out, and a prize can be awarded to the pair with the most.

5   The following questions can be used after telling the tale to lead into a discussion: Have you ever been conned (taken advantage of) like the king was in the story or do you know anybody who has been badly tricked? How are tourists deceived in London or the city where you live? Tell me about it.

CRAB: WORKSHEET

Work in pairs. Ask each other the following questions, then report back with your findings:

a. How superstitious are you? Give examples of superstitions that you or people from your country believe in?

b. How often do you read your horoscope and what can you tell me about your zodiac sign?

c. Have you ever been to a fortune-teller? Tell me about the experience.

d. If you had a personal problem, who or what would you consult for help, and why?

Read through the story to find words which mean the same as the following:

a. he made an official announcement

b. but made up his mind

c. That is for you to decide

d. from the critical look in the peasant's eyes

e. they were frightened they would be discovered

f. only addressed him as

g. informs the king that we are the culprits

h. there is no hope for us

i. request that he does not inform on us

j. How did you manage to get yourself in such a mess?

We learn from the story that Crab could neither read nor write. What other situations can you think of in which being illiterate could be an advantage? Work in pairs or small groups and make a list of them.

Now match the numbers with the letters to complete these proverbs about crime and punishment:

1. Crime   a. don't make a right.
2. Honesty   b. doesn't pay.
3. To err   c. fit the crime.
4. Two wrongs   d. is above the law.
5. It takes a thief   e. is fair in love and war.
6. Let the punishment   f. is human, to forgive is divine.
7. Justice   g. is the best policy.
8. Cheats   h. must be done, and must be seen to be done.
9. Nobody   i. never prosper.
10. All   j. to catch a thief.

CRAB

There was once a king who had lost a valuable ring. He looked for it everywhere, but could not find it. So he issued a proclamation that if any astrologer could tell him where it was he would be richly rewarded. A poor peasant by the name of Crab heard of the proclamation. He could neither read nor write, but took it into his head that he wanted to be the astrologer to find the king's ring.

So he went and presented himself to the king, to whom he said: "Your Majesty must know that I am an astrologer although you see me so poorly dressed. I know that you have lost a ring and I will try by study to find out where it is." "Very well," said the king, "and when you have found it, what reward must I give you?" "That is at your discretion, your Majesty." "Go, then, study, and we shall see what kind of an astrologer you turn out to be."

He was conducted to a room, in which he was to be shut up to study. It contained only a bed and a table on which were a large book and writing materials. Crab seated himself at the table and did nothing but turn over the leaves of the book and scribble on the paper so that the servants who brought him his food thought him a great man. They were the ones who had stolen the ring, and from the severe glances that the peasant cast at them whenever they entered, they began to fear that they would be found out. They made him endless bows and never opened their mouths without calling him "Mr. Astrologer." Crab, who, although illiterate, was, as a peasant, cunning, all at once imagined that the servants must know about the ring, and this is the way his suspicions were confirmed He had been shut up in his room turning over his big book and scribbling his paper for a month, when his wife came to visit him. He said to her: "Hide yourself under the bed, and when a servant enters, say: 'That is one'; when another comes, say: 'That is two'; and so on."

The woman hid herself. The servants came with the dinner, and hardly had the first one entered when a voice from under the bed said: "That is one." The second one entered; the voice said: "That is two"; and so on. The servants were frightened at hearing that voice, for they did not know where it came from, and held a consultation.

One of them said: "We are discovered; if the astrologer denounces us to the king as thieves, we are lost."

"Do you know what we must do?" said another.

"Let us hear."

"We must go to the astrologer and tell him frankly that we stole the ring, and ask him not to betray us, and present him with a purse of money. Are you willing?"

"Perfectly."

So they went in harmony to the astrologer, and making him a lower bow than usual, one of them began: "Mr. Astrologer, you have discovered that we stole the ring. We are poor people and if you reveal it to the king, we are undone. So we beg you not to betray us, and accept this purse of money." Crab took the purse and then added: "I will not betray you, but you must do what I tell you, if you wish to save your lives. Take the ring and make that turkey in the courtyard swallow it, and leave the rest to me." The servants were satisfied to do so and departed with a low bow. The next day Crab went to the king and said to him: "Your Majesty must know that after having toiled over a month I have succeeded in discovering where the ring has gone to." Where is it, then?"

asked the king. "A turkey has swallowed it." "A turkey? Very well, let us see."

They went for the turkey, opened it, and found the ring inside. The king, amazed, presented the astrologer with a large purse of money and invited him to a banquet. Among the other dishes, there was brought on the table a plate of crabs. Crabs must then have been very rare, because only the king and a few others knew their name. Turning to the peasant the king said: "You, who are an astrologer, must be able to tell me the name of these things which are in this dish." The poor astrologer was very much puzzled, and, as if speaking to himself, but in such a way that the others heard him, he muttered: "Ah! Crab, Crab, what a plight you are in!" All who did not know that his name was Crab rose and proclaimed him the greatest astrologer in the world.

(taken from *Best-Loved Folktales of The World* selected by Joanna Cole, Anchor Books 1982)

THE BATTLE BETWEEN GOOD AND EVIL

Level: Upper Intermediate

Target Audience: Secondary / Adults

Language / Skills Focus: Listening & Speaking

Materials: Photocopies of the worksheet

IN CLASS

1. Pre-Listening: *The story is called* The Battle between Good and Evil. *Ask the learners to predict who is likely to win the battle, and why?*
2. "When have you been tempted by evil, and what was the outcome? Tell the person sitting next to you about it."
3. *Post-Listening:* "What do you think you would have done if you had been Ahab and St Savin had come visiting you?"
4. "Think of an event that has happened to you that resulted in you making a significant change to your life. Tell the person sitting next to you about it."
5. Hand out copies of the worksheet and invite the learners to work on the activities in pairs or small groups.

    Match the numbers on the left with the letters on the right to find explanations for the new language in the story: 1-d / 2-n / 3-f / 4-a / 5-c / 6-m / 7-l / 8-b / 9-e / 10-j / 11-g / 12- k / 13-o / 14-h / 15-i

    True or False 1-F / 2-T / 3-T / 4-T / 5-F / 6-T / 7-F / 8- T / 9- T

The final activity on the worksheet is designed to lead into a discussion:

"Hear no _____, see no _____, and speak no _____ ." The same missing word is repeated three times in this expression. What is the missing word, and is the warning a sensible one? Or do you think it's better to tell the truth at all times, regardless of what the consequences might be? Discuss what you think in pairs or small groups, and then elect a spokesperson to report back the rest of the class with your findings.

COMMENTS

The story is based on an anecdote in *The Devil and Miss Prym* by Paolo Coelho published by Harper Collins 2001.

THE BATTLE BETWEEN GOOD AND EVIL: WORKSHEET

Match the numbers on the left with the letters on the right to find explanations for the new language in the story:

1.	abandoned	a.	criminals who deceive people
2.	bandits	b.	crying
3.	chatted	c.	escaping / running away
4.	confidence tricksters	d.	gave up
5.	fleeing	e.	in a threatening manner
6.	a frontier post	f.	made conversation
7.	a hermit	g.	make a long cut with a sharp knife
8.	in tears	h.	morally offensive
9.	menacingly	i.	most evil
10.	prostitutes	j.	people who have sex for money
11.	slit	k.	people who take things illegally into another country
12.	smugglers	l.	somebody who chooses to live alone, away from other people
13.	uneasy	m.	the border between two countries
14.	unsavoury	n.	thieves who attack travellers in wild places
15.	wickedest	o.	worried that something bad might happen

True or False

1. St Savin lived in a cave because he had no money.
2. The village was on the border of another country.
3. It was notorious for harbouring criminals.
4. Ahab admitted that he was a murderer.
5. St Savin wanted to stay in his house because he was tired of living in a cave.
6. Although Ahab agreed to let him stay for the night, his plan was to kill him.
7. Savin was crying the next morning because he'd fallen asleep and missed his chance.
8. Ahab repaid St Savin's willingness to trust him by sparing his life.
9. From that day on Ahab never committed another crime.

"Hear no _____, see no _____, and speak no _____." The same missing word is repeated three times in this expression. What is the missing word, and is the warning a sensible one? Or do you think it's better to tell the truth at all times, regardless of what the consequences might be? Discuss what you think in pairs or small groups, and then elect a spokesperson to report back the rest of the class with your findings.

THE BATTLE BETWEEN GOOD AND EVIL

Once upon a time, a hermit – who later came to be known as St Savin – lived in a cave in the mountains above a village.

The village, a frontier post, was a dreadful place, populated by all sorts of unsavoury characters - bandits fleeing from justice, smugglers, prostitutes, confidence tricksters, even murderers resting between murders. And the wickedest of them all was an Arab called Ahab.

One day Savin came down from his cave, arrived at Ahab's house and asked to spend the night there. Ahab laughed: "You do know that I'm a murderer who has already slit a number of throats, and that your life is worth nothing to me?"

"Yes, I know that," Savin replied, "but I'm tired of living in a cave and I'd like to spend at least one night here with you."

Ahab knew the saint's reputation, which was as great as his own, and this made him feel uneasy. So he determined to kill him that very night, to prove to everyone that he was the one true master of the place.

They chatted for a while and Ahab was impressed by what the man had to say. But Ahab was a suspicious man who no longer believed in the existence of Good. He showed Savin where he could sleep and then continued menacingly sharpening his knife. After watching him for a few minutes, Savin closed his eyes and went to sleep.

Ahab spent all night sharpening his knife. The next day, when Savin woke up, he found Ahab in tears at his side.

"You weren't afraid of me and you didn't judge me. For the first time ever, someone spent a night by my side trusting that I could be a good man, one ready to offer hospitality to those in need. And because you believed I was capable of behaving decently, I did."

From that moment on, the king of the bandits abandoned his life of crime, never to return to it again.

THE WEDDING AT STANTON DREW

Level: Advanced

Target Audience: Adults

Language / Skills Focus: Listening, Speaking & Writing

Materials: Photocopies of the story (optional) to hand out at the end of the session.

IN CLASS

The following questions could be used to provide a lead-in to the story: Describe a typical wedding in your country. What kind of wedding would you like to have if you got married?

During the while listening stage, pause after "a long venerable beard" Ask the learners to predict what follows: Who do you think the stranger is? You can also pause after "frozen solid with horror" to ask the following question: What do you think the guests at the wedding saw?

As a post-listening activity, the learners can produce a sequel to the story entitled *The Fiend Returns*, working in small groups. Each group should choose someone to write out the story and someone to read it to the rest of the class. You can circulate to provide any assistance required during the composition stage, making a note of the effective language used as well as any errors that crop up and these can be dealt with at the end of the session

The following questions could then be used to lead the class into a discussion: Are the standing stones at Stanton Drew really the frozen guests from the wedding or an ancient ceremonial site? What do you think? Do you have any sites like this in your country with legends about their origin?

Then, if time allows, photocopies of the story can be handed out and the dialogue writing activity can be set up.

COMMENTS

Stanton Drew is a large set of three stone circles, south of Bristol. The Great Circle is the second largest stone circle in England, after Avebury, with 27 stones. The tale is about a wedding which started off as a joyous occasion but turned into a tragedy. It is adapted from a story found in *English Folk Tales* by Sybil Marshall, Orion Books Ltd, 1996.

THE WEDDING AT STANTON DREW

At the sweet time of the year when spring slips unnoticed into summer, when the swallows are back and buttercups yellow the fields, when evening dusk merges into mellow moonlight, and the night is almost as warm as the day, it is the right time for weddings - especially in a village where everything keeps tune with the rhythm of the seasons. So it was at Stanton Drew, a tiny village on the banks of the river Chew in Somerset, many, many years ago. The day was a balmy Saturday, when the bride and the groom and all their family and friends walked to the church for the marriage ceremony and the blessing of the priest. That over, they set about the business of enjoying themselves, and making the most of the occasion, with eating, drinking, and the romping merriment of music and dance.

When early evening came, the local harpist came too; and out into a field close by the church the wedding party went, to take their places for the age-old country dances in which grace and elegance give way to strength and agility, and the figures only stop when dancers and musicians alike run out of breath.

As dance succeeded dance, the party grew merrier and merrier, and the feet of the company more nimble. None was more nimble than the bride, whose sparkling eyes and rosy cheeks grew ever more excited and whose laughter rang ever more loud and abandoned.

The moon was high, the night was calm, and time slipped by as if on magic wings. They were in the very middle of a dance when the harpist suddenly drew his fingers across the strings with a firm chord, and the music drifted into silence. The dancers stood waiting for him to continue, but they could see that he was making preparations to pack up.

The bride left her place in the figure and ran across to him. 'What's the matter?' she asked. 'Why are you stopping?'

He pointed up to the moon. 'It's time to stop,' he said. 'It's now midnight, and in a few minutes it will be the Sabbath Day.'

'What does that matter?' said the excited girl. 'I'm only going to get married once, and I'm going to dance all night if I want to!'

The pious old musician was shocked. 'Then you'll have to find somebody else to play for you,' he answered.

Then the bride pleaded, and coaxed, and cajoled to prevail on him to stay; but he shook his head, and prepared to leave. At this the girl flew into a passion, and her pleadings turned to abuse. 'Go then, you miserable old spoilsport,' she yelled. 'We'll dance without you and your music! I'll find somebody else to play for one more dance, if I have to go to Hell to get him!'

As the old man shuffled off towards home in the moonlight, the angry shouts of the disappointed revellers followed him into the night; and as they turned dejectedly to follow him, since they could not dance without music, they saw approaching from the opposite way the outline of a stranger. He came upon them out of the night, and they saw that he was old, but most impressive looking, with exceedingly bright eyes and a long venerable beard.

'Greetings to you!' he said pleasantly. 'I heard the sounds of a quarrel as I came towards you. Now what can be wrong with a merry party on such a beautiful night?'

Then the bride, in tears of anger, told the courteous old stranger how the harpist with his religious scruples had taken himself off at midnight, and put an end to all their fun.

'If that's the only problem, it can soon be solved,' said the old man. 'I'll play for you myself.' And he sat down on a convenient boulder, took a pipe from under his cloak, and began to play.

It seemed at first that his fingers were stiff and out of practice, but he soon caught up the rhythm again, and choosing their partners for a round dance, they began to move to his music. After a minute or two, he began to quicken his tempo, and the dancers felt their feet responding to the urgent music in a way they had never done before with their familiar harpist. Faster and faster the new musician played, and faster and faster they whirled, till the peace of the holy Sabbath was shattered with their wild laughter and cries of merriment. On and on went the music, and on and on went the dance, until all were breathless and exhausted, and longing to sit down and rest.

'Stop!' cried the bride, gasping for air. 'Stop and let us rest.' The piper, however, took no notice, so they decided to stop of their own accord and fling themselves down on the grass to recover. It was then they found out that they had no control over their feet at all, and that while the music went on, they had no option but to go on dancing to it. Seeing their predicament, the piper lifted his head, and played louder, and stronger, and faster, faster, ever faster, till the gasps of the dancers turned to moans, and their merry cries to groans, and their laughter to wails as their pleas for mercy died away for lack of breath with which to utter them. Still the relentless music went on, and still their feet rose and fell in time with it, hour after hour as the night wore on, and the moon sank, leaving them still dancing in the darkness.

At last the first streaks of dawn began to show in the eastern sky, and faint hope began to rise in their hearts that with the new day their terrible ordeal must end. So it proved, for as the first rays of the morning sun struck him, their strange musician put down his pipe and stood up. The circle of exhausted dancers immediately stopped in their tracks, and stood as if frozen solid with horror! For protruding from beneath his robe was an unmistakable cloven hoof, from under his hood they spied a pair of unmistakable horns, and behind him they saw the end of an unmistakable forked tail. While they stood as if petrified with terror, he put away his pipe and turned towards them.

'I'll come back and play for you again, one day,' he chuckled, and walked away into the morning. Then as they watched the Devil depart, for that is surely who he was, they turned into pillars of stone where they stood.

There they stand to this very day, the inner circle of three sets of standing stones, in a field close by the church at Stanton Drew; and there they will stay, it is supposed, until the Fiend returns to play for them again, as he promised to do all those many centuries ago, when knowingly they chose to break the Sabbath for the sake of one more dance.

How many of these proverbs and expressions do you know?

Talk of the devil! / I'll keep my fingers crossed. / You haven't got the ghost of a chance! / It scared the hell out of me! / She's determined to finish the job come hell or high water. / He was between the devil and the deep blue sea. / I can feel it in my bones. / She's got the luck of the devil! / Someone's just walked over my grave. / He seems to have given up the ghost on this job. / Better the Devil you know than the Devil you don't / Everybody wants to go to heaven but nobody wants to die The Devil finds work for idle hands to do / There but for the grace of God go you or I

Now, working in pairs, make dialogues using as many of the proverbs and expressions as you can. When you are ready, be prepared to read out your dialogue to the rest of the class, who will count up how many you have used from the list and check to see whether you have used them correctly or not. And the couple with the highest number will win a fabulous mystery prize!

THE GIRL WHO WAS LOVED BY A TREE SPIRIT

Level: Upper Intermediate / Advanced

Target Audience: Secondary / Adults

Language / Skills Focus: Listening / Speaking / Writing

Materials: Photocopies of the worksheet. Photocopies of the story (optional) to hand out at the end of the session.

IN CLASS

1. *Pre-listening:* You could start the lesson with a brainstorming session to find out how much the learners already know about the subject – by questioning them on the superstitions or folk stories about trees from their own countries.

2. *Post-listening:* Hand out copies of the worksheet for the students to work on in pairs.

   Match the numbers on the left with the letters on the right to find explanations for the new vocabulary: 1-o / 2-i / 3-l / 4-c / 5-k / 6-n / 7-e / 8-g / 9-d / 10-q / 11-p / 12-a / 13-r / 14-h / 15-j / 16-f / 17-b / 18-m

3. Using the category of water, invite everyone in the group to write on a slip of paper what kind of water they would like to be – river, ocean, waterfall, pond, icicle, cloud, tear, raindrop etc. These slips are put in an envelope, shuffled around, and then read out by someone from the group. The other group members can then make suggestions like I think ..... would like to be a waterfall because ... If the suggestion is correct, the writer acknowledges the fact. The aim of the activity is for the participants to share perceptions of each other, which can help develop trust.

4. "On the advice of her parents, she tied a new belt around her lover's waist one night." Invite the learners to make a list of all the things they have done on the advice of their parents, and to reflect on how many of them have turned out to be in their best interests. They can then share their experiences in small groups, and each group can elect a spokesperson to report back their findings to the rest of the class.

5. Ask the learners, working in small groups, to write parallel stories making use of the following titles: *The Girl Who Was Loved By A Mountain Spirit / The Girl Who Was Loved By A Water Spirit / The Girl Who Was Loved By A Star Spirit / The Girl Who Was Loved By A Cloud Spirit / The Girl Who Was Loved By A Fire Spirit*

THE GIRL WHO WAS LOVED BY A TREE SPIRIT

In Chungliyimti village there once lived a beautiful girl, the daughter of a rich family. Many young men came to her dormitory at night to court her. But she gave all her attention to one particular young man, the most handsome of them all. He came to her every night and went away before dawn. But he could never be found during the daytime. The girl looked for him among the village bachelors in the fields, in people's private houses, and in many other places. But her search was always in vain. At last she reported her experiences to her father and mother. On the advice of her parents, she tied a new belt around her lover's waist one night. He departed with it at the usual time. To the girl's surprise, when she went out for a walk the next morning, she found the belt tied around a tree that was standing below her house near the bank of a stream. The family now began to suspect that the young man was not a human being at all but the spirit of that tree.

To confirm their suspicions, the girl put an indigo-dyed shawl on the man's shoulders the following night in the same manner as she had tied the belt on him during his previous visit. He departed as usual. In the morning they found that same shawl hanging from a forked branch of the special tree. It stood near the edge of a well where the girl often went for water. Then the daughter remembered that she had gone to that well often during the period of courtship with her lover. She had washed her hands, and legs, and face daily and had liked to sing as she bathed. She now remembered that the branches of the tree above her used to move up and down, as if blown by the wind, whenever she came to that spot and realised that the spirit of this particular tree had come to court her in the form of a handsome bachelor.

The girl's father soon decided to see these mysterious happenings for himself and so kept a watch one night outside the girl's dormitory. When the stranger left before dawn, he secretly followed him. Instead of going to the young man's dormitory, as all the other youths did, this man went straight to the stream. There he stood at the side of the well and quickly transformed himself into an ordinary tree. His body turned into the trunk, his arms into branches, and his hair into leaves.

The father then decided to cut this mysterious tree down. He called the villagers together and asked their help in felling it, after telling the whole story to explain his concern. He also asked his daughter to remain inside the house, just in case anything dangerous happened. The men cut and cut, but the tree would not fall. And as they chopped, a small chip of wood flew toward the girl's house. At that very moment the girl was watching the cutters by peeping through a small hole in the wall. The flying wood chip entered the hole and struck her in the eye. It moved with such speed that it damaged her brain and the girl died instantly.

At the same moment that the girl fell to the floor, the tree also fell with a huge crash. The father was now happy. He came home rejoicing, relieved at the thought that the tree spirit would no longer chase and haunt his lovely daughter. To his utter shock and horror, he found his daughter dead. The two lovers had died together.

THE GIRL WHO WAS LOVED BY A TREE SPIRIT: WORKSHEET

Match the numbers on the left with the letters on the right to find explanations for the new vocabulary:

1.	bachelors	a blue-purple colour
2.	chase	b. a cloth worn by a woman around her shoulders
3.	chip	c. cut into small pieces
4.	chopped	d. cutting down (a tree)
5.	confirm their suspicions	e. early morning when light first appears in the sky
6.	courtship	f. feeling happy because something bad didn't happen
7.	dawn	g. a large room with lots of beds
8.	dormitory	h. looking at something secretly
9.	felling	i. run after
10.	haunt	j. showing great happiness
11.	huge	k. show what they think to be true
12.	indigo	l. a small piece that has broken off something
13.	in vain	m. the thick part of a tree that the branches grow from
14.	peeping	n. the time a couple spend together before they marry
15.	rejoicing	o. unmarried men
16.	relieved	p. very big
17.	shawl	q. visit often
18.	trunk	r. without success

"On the advice of her parents, she tied a new belt around her lover's waist one night." Make a list of all the things you have done on the advice of your parents. How many of them have turned out to be good for you? Share your experiences in small groups, and then elect a spokesperson to report back on your behalf to the rest of the class.

What other stories do you know about shape-shifting – people or animals that change from one form into another? Working in small groups, write a parallel story using of one of the following titles:

The Girl Who Was Loved By A Mountain Spirit / The Girl Who Was Loved By A Water Spirit / The Girl Who Was Loved By A Star Spirit / The Girl Who Was Loved By A Cloud Spirit

THE TOAD BRIDEGROOM

Level: Upper Intermediate / Advanced
Target Audience: Secondary / Adults
Language / Skills Focus: Listening / Speaking / Writing
Materials: Photocopies of the worksheet. Photocopies of the story (optional) to hand out at the end of the session.

IN CLASS

The story raises some interesting questions, especially if the character of the toad is replaced by someone with physical disabilities or special needs. For example, how would you react if your son / daughter wanted to marry a paraplegic? Would you support or try to discourage them from taking such a step?

Pre-listening: You might like to start with a brainstorming session, to find out what the listeners already know about toads.

Post-listening: Would you be prepared to marry someone that everyone else was likely to disapprove of or would you be prepared to let one of your children take such a step? What could you do in an effort to put an end to such a relationship? The toad refused to accept no as an answer. The more he was rejected, the more determined he became. Would you have been as determined as he was?

In the past, young people often had no choice as marriages were arranged. In fact, they still are today in some countries. How do you feel about arranged marriages? Are they more or less likely to be successful? What do you think? "Are You Ruled By Your Heart Or Your Head?" After pre-teaching new vocabulary, arrange the students in groups. Hand out a copy of the questionnaire to an "interviewer" in each group who reads the questions to the other students and takes on the role of the teacher. Only the interviewer should be able to see the copy and he/she presents the questionnaire to the group as a listening activity. Meanwhile, you can circulate to provide any assistance required. The next stage is for the students to add up their scores and assess the results, which can be examined and discussed by the class as a whole. Although the material is inauthentic in that the questionnaire is contrived, the students have an authentic reason for doing the activity – to find out more about themselves.

Write an account of (or tell the other people in your group about) a love story with a happy ending – real or imaginary.

COMMENTS

Nothing and no one can stand in the way of true love, especially with a little help from above, as this version of *The Frog King* shows. This particular example of the story, which can be found in many different cultures, has been adapted from a traditional Korean tale.

THE TOAD BRIDEGROOM

Long ago there lived a poor fisherman in a certain village. One day he went fishing in the lake as usual, but found he could not catch as many fish as he was accustomed to. And on each of the following days he found his catch growing smaller and smaller. He tried new baits, and bought new hooks, but all to no avail. At last even the water of the lake began to disappear, until in the end it became too shallow for fishing.

One afternoon in the late summer the bottom of the lake was exposed to view, and a big toad came out from it. The fisherman immediately thought that it must have eaten up all the fish and angrily cursed the creature. Then the toad spoke to him gently, rolling its eyes, "Don't be angry because one day I'll bring you good fortune. I want to live in your house, so please let me go with you." But the fisherman was annoyed that a toad should make such a request and went home without it.

That evening the toad came to his house. His wife, who had already heard about it from her husband, received it kindly, and made a bed for it in a corner of the kitchen. Then she brought it worms and scraps to eat. The couple had no children of their own, and decided to keep the toad as a pet. It grew to be as big as a boy, and they came to love it as if it were their son.

Nearby there lived a rich man who had three daughters. One day the toad told the fisherman and his wife that it would like to marry one of the three daughters. They were most alarmed at this most unreasonable request and earnestly advised it to forget such an impossible ambition. "It's utterly absurd," they said. "How can poor people like us propose marriage to such a great family? And you aren't even a human being!"

So the toad replied, "I don't care what the rank of the family is. The parents may object, but one of the daughters may be willing to accept me. Who knows? Please go and ask, and let me know what answer you receive."

So the fisherman's wife went and called on the mistress of the rich man's house and told her what her toad-son had asked. The lady was greatly displeased and went and told her husband. He was absolutely furious too at such a preposterous suggestion and ordered his servant to beat the toad's foster-mother. So the poor woman returned home and told the toad of her painful experience.

"I'm very sorry that you have been treated like that, Mother," the toad said to her, "but don't let it worry you too much. Just wait and see what will happen." Then he went out and caught a hawk and brought it home. Late that night he tied a lighted lantern to its foot, and crept stealthily to the rich man's house. He tied a long string to the hawk's foot and then climbed a tall tree that stood by the house. Then he held the end of the string in his hand and released the hawk to fly over the house.

As it flew into the air he solemnly declared in a loud voice, "The master of this house shall listen to my words, for I have been dispatched by the Heavenly King. Today you rejected a proposal of marriage, and now you shall be punished for your arrogance. I'll give you one day to reconsider your decision. I advise you to accept the toad's proposal, for if you don't, you, your brothers, and your children shall be utterly destroyed."

The people in the house were startled by this nocturnal proclamation from the sky, and they opened the windows to see what was going on. When they looked up into the sky they saw a dim light hovering overhead. The master of the house went out into the garden and kneeled humbly on the ground looking up into the sky. Then the toad let go of the string he held in his hand, and the hawk soared skywards with the lantern still tied to its foot. The rich man was now convinced that what he had heard was spoken by a messenger from Heaven, and at once resolved to consent to the toad's marriage to one of his daughters.

Next morning the rich man went and called on the toad's foster parents, and apologized humbly for his discourteous refusal on the previous day. He said now that he would gladly accept the toad as his son-in-law. Then he returned home and asked his eldest daughter to marry the toad, but she rushed from the room in fury and humiliation. Then he called his second daughter, and suggested that she be the toad's wife, but she too rushed from the room without a word. So he called his youngest daughter and explained to her that if she refused she would place the whole family in a most difficult position indeed, so stern had been the warning from Heaven. But the youngest daughter agreed to marry the toad without the slightest hesitation.

The wedding took place on the following day, and a great crowd of guests attended consumed by curiosity at such an unusual happening. That night, when they retired, the toad asked his bride to bring him a pair of scissors. She went and got a pair, and then he asked her to cut the skin off his back. This strange request startled her greatly, but he insisted that she do so without delay, and so she made a long cut in his back. Then, lo and behold, a handsome young man stepped out of the skin.

In the morning the bridegroom put on his toad skin again, so that nobody noticed any difference. Her two sisters sneered contemptuously at the bride with her repulsive husband, but she took no notice of them. At noon all the men of the household went out on horseback with bows and arrows to hunt. The toad accompanied them on foot and unarmed. But the party had no success in the hunt and had to return empty-handed.

The bridegroom stripped off his toad skin and became a man when they had gone, and waved his hand in the air. Then a white-haired old man appeared and he told him to bring one hundred deer. When the deer came he drove them homeward, once more wearing his toad skin. Everyone was most surprised to see all the deer, and then he suddenly stripped off the toad skin and revealed himself as a handsome young man, at which their astonishment knew no bounds. Then he released all the deer and rose up to Heaven, carrying his bride on his back and his parents on his arms.

TOAD BRIDEGROOM: WORKSHEET

Are you ruled by your Heart or your Head?

1. What would you rather be known as?
   a. a sympathetic person b. an intelligent person

2. Which qualities do you value in a friend?
   a. support and love b. common sense and practical advice

3. When can you tell you're in love?
   a. when you realise someone has the qualities you're looking for
   b. when you heart beats faster and you go weak at the knees

4. Which bits do you like best when reading a newspaper?
   a. the news and the crossword
   b. romantic short stories and the agony aunt page

5. What do you believe we should teach children?
   a. how to listen to other people b. how to win arguments

6. What's your favourite kind of music?
   a. poetic and intellectual b. sentimental and romantic

7. What sort of books do you prefer reading?
   a. detective whodunits b. historic romances

8. What would your ideal job be?
   a. a lawyer or a politician b. a nurse or a musician

9. How do you judge a person's character?
   a. by following your feelings b. by analysing the way they behave

10. What are you more likely to do if you know telling the truth will hurt someone's feelings?
    a. tell a white lie b. be brutally honest

ANSWERS

1. a-1 b-2	6. a-1 b-2
2. a-1 b-2	7. a-2 b-1
3. a-2 b-1	8. a-2 b-1
4. a-2 b-1	9. a-1 b-2
5. a-1 b-2	10. a-1 b-2

WHAT YOUR SCORE MEANS:

15-20 You're an analytical kind of person with strong principles and insist on being treated fairly. However, you have a tendency to hurt other people by being thoughtless and you should listen to your feelings more often.

10-14 You need praise and love. You're a good listener and like to please other people. Sometimes though, you're too passionate for your own good and act without thinking first. Try to introduce an element of balance into your decision-making.

THE MIRROR OF MATSUYAMA

Level: Upper Intermediate
Target Audience: Adults
Language / Skills Focus: Listening & Speaking
Materials: Photocopies of the worksheet

IN CLASS

1. *Pre-listening:* The story is about a mirror. What do you suppose is special about it? Now listen to find out if you guessed correctly.

2. *While-listening:* Pause after the words "if she behaved herself while he was away …" and ask the learners to predict the ending to the sentence.

3. *Post-listening*: If you'd been the father, would you have been capable of suspecting your daughter of practising witchcraft? If you'd been the daughter, would you have forgiven the stepmother?

4. Match the numbers on the left with the letters on the right to find explanations for the new vocabulary: 1-g / 2-c / 3-j / 4-k / 5-b / 6-d / 7-m / 8-o / 9-n / 10-l / 11-h / 12-i / 13-e / 14-q / 15-p / 16-f / 17-r / 18-a

5. Working in pairs, ask each other the following questions, then report back to the rest of the class with your findings:
   a. What's the most special present that you've ever been given, and why?
   b. What possessions do you have that are of particular sentimental value to you?
   c. What other stories about magical mirrors do you know?
   d. How much time do you spend looking in the mirror?
   e. The next time you look into a mirror, who or what would like to see?

6. In a mixed nationality class, the answers to the following questions can be shared in pairs or small groups: In Japan, *The Mirror of Matsuyama* was traditionally told at *Hinamatsuri* (the Girls' Festival), on March 3rd. In England, Guy Fawkes Night is celebrated on November 5th and the story of the Gunpowder Plot is told. What festivals are celebrated in your country each year, and what stories are associated with them?

COMMENTS

The Mirror of Matsuyama has been adapted from a story in *Myths and Legends of Japan* by F. Hadland Davis, George G. Harrap and Company, 1917.

THE MIRROR OF MATSUYAMA

In a remote part of Japan there lived a man and his wife who were blessed with a little girl they loved dearly. On one occasion the man was called away on business to distant Kyoto. Before he went he told his daughter that if she behaved herself while he was away, he would bring her back a special present. Then the good man took his departure.

At last he returned to his home, and after his wife and child had taken off his large hat and sandals he sat down upon the white mats and opened a bamboo basket, watching the eager gaze of his little child. He took out a wonderful doll and a lacquer box of cakes and put them into her outstretched hands. He then presented his wife with a metal mirror. Its surface shone brightly and on the back there was a design of pine trees and storks.

The good man's wife had never seen a mirror before, and on gazing into it she was under the impression that another woman looked out upon her. Her husband explained the mystery and instructed her to take great care of the mirror.

Not long after this happy homecoming the woman became very ill. Just before she died she called to her little daughter, and said: "You're going to miss me when I'm gone but you've got to be strong. And I want you to take this mirror. Whenever you feel lonely look into it and you'll always see me." Having said these words she passed away.

In due time the man married again, and his wife was not at all kind to her stepdaughter. But the little one, remembering her mother's words, would look into the mirror, where it seemed to her that she saw her dear mother's face again, not drawn in pain as she had seen it on her deathbed, but young and beautiful.

One day this child's stepmother chanced to see her crouching in a corner over an object she could not quite see, murmuring to herself. This ignorant woman, who detested the child and believed that her stepdaughter detested her in return, fancied that this little one was performing some strange magical art - perhaps making an image and sticking pins into it. Full of these notions, the stepmother went to her husband and told him that his wicked child was doing her best to kill her by witchcraft.

When the master of the house had listened to this extraordinary accusation, he went straight to his daughter's room to speak to her about it. He took her by surprise, and immediately the girl saw him she slipped the mirror into her sleeve. For the first time her doting father grew angry, and he feared that there was, after all, truth in what his wife had told him.

When his daughter had heard this unjust accusation she was amazed at her father's words. She told him that she loved him far too much ever to attempt to kill his wife, especially as she knew how much he loved her.

"What have you hidden in your sleeve?" said her father, only half convinced and still extremely puzzled.

"The mirror you gave my mother, and which she on her deathbed gave to me. Every time I look into its shining surface I see the face of my dear mother, young and beautiful. When my heart aches, I take out the mirror, and mother's face, with her sweet, kind smile, brings me peace, and helps me to keep on going."

Then the man understood and loved his child even more for the strength of character she had shown. Even the girl's stepmother, when she knew what had really taken place, was ashamed and asked forgiveness. And this child, who believed she had seen her mother's face in the mirror, forgave, and trouble forever departed from the home.

THE MIRROR OF MATSUYAMA: WORKSHEET

Match the numbers on the left with the letters on the right to find explanations for the new vocabulary:

1.	remote	a.	confused
2.	eager	b.	died
3.	storks	c.	enthusiastic
4.	gazing	d.	eventually
5.	passed away	e.	evil
6.	in due time	f.	extremely loving and caring
7.	chanced to see	g.	far away
8.	crouching	h.	hated
9.	murmuring	i.	ideas
10.	ignorant	j.	large white birds, with long legs
11.	detested	k.	looking for a long time
12.	notions	l.	not having enough knowledge
13.	wicked	m.	saw by accident
14.	witchcraft	n.	speaking quietly so you can only be heard by someone near
15.	sleeve	o.	staying close to the ground by bending your knees
16.	doting	p.	the part of a shirt or jacket that covers the arm
17.	unjust	q.	the practice of magic
18.	puzzled	r.	unfair

Working in pairs, ask each other the following questions, then report back to the rest of the class with your findings:

a. What's the most special present that you've ever been given, and why?
b. What possessions do you have that are of particular sentimental value to you?
c. What other stories about magical mirrors do you know?
d. How much time do you spend looking in the mirror?
e. The next time you look into a mirror, who or what would like to see?

In Japan, *The Mirror of Matsuyama* was traditionally told at *Hinamatsuri* (the Girls' Festival), on March 3rd. In England, Guy Fawkes Night is celebrated on November 5th and the story of the Gunpowder Plot is told. What festivals are celebrated in your country each year, and what stories are associated with them?

HOW BUTTERFLIES CAME TO BE

Level: Upper Intermediate - Advanced
Target Audience: Adults
Language / Skills Focus: Listening, Speaking & Writing
Materials: Photocopies of the worksheet. Photocopies of the story (optional) to hand out at the end of the session.

IN CLASS

1. As a pre-listening activity, ask the learners to find the answers to these questions:
   a. What saddened the Creator when he watched the children playing?
   b. What did he make the butterflies from?
   c. Why did he take the songs away from the butterflies?

2. The matching activity can be completed by the learners individually or in pairs. Invite whoever finishes early up to the front to board their answers so as to avoid teacher-centred feedback. 1-e / 2-j / 3-f / 4-g / 5-b / 6-h / 7-j / 8-a / 9-i /10-c / 11-d

3. The quotation from the story that is presented here and the questions that follow it can be used to lead into a discussion: "These children will grow old and their skin will become wrinkled. Their hair will turn grey and their teeth will fall out. The young hunter's arm will fail and these lovely young girls will grow fat and ugly". How concerned are you about the signs of ageing? Would you ever consider having cosmetic surgery done? Why or why not? Do you know anybody who has had cosmetic surgery? What were the results like? These are all questions you might like to discuss in small groups. A spokesperson for the group can then be elected to report your findings to the rest of the class.

4. *Why did the Creator make the other creatures that inhabit the Earth?* Arrange the learners into small groups and invite each group to choose another creature to write a story about. Possible titles could include How Giraffes Came To Be / How Camels Came To Be / How Dalmations Came To Be etc.

5. Now match the numbers with the letters to complete these proverbs about animals: 1-d / 2-c / 3-l / 4-j / 5-f / 6-b / 7-h / 8-k / 9-e / 10-g / 11-a / 12-i

COMMENTS

The story is a Native American creation myth. It celebrates the differences between us, which help to make the world such a colourful and interesting place. Like many such tales, it is ideal as a lead-in to parallel story writing.

HOW BUTTERFLIES CAME TO BE

One day the Creator was resting, watching some children at play in a village. The children laughed and sang, yet as he watched them, the Creator's heart was sad. He was thinking: "These children will grow old and their skin will become wrinkled. Their hair will turn grey and their teeth will fall out. The young hunter's arm will fail and these lovely young girls will grow fat and ugly. The playful puppies will become blind, mangy dogs. And those wonderful flowers-yellow and blue, red and purple-will fade. The leaves from the trees will fall and dry up. Already they are turning yellow." Thus the Creator grew sadder and sadder. It was in the autumn, and the thought of the coming winter, with its cold and lack of game and green things, made his heart heavy.

Yet it was still warm, and the sun was shining. The Creator watched the play of sunlight and shadow on the ground, the yellow leaves being carried here and there by the wind. He saw the blueness of the sky, the whiteness of some cornmeal ground by the women. Suddenly he smiled. "All those colors, they ought to be preserved. I'll make something to gladden my heart, something for these children to look at and enjoy."

The Creator took out his bag and started gathering things: a spot of sunlight, a handful of blue from the sky, the whiteness of the cornmeal, the shadow of playing children, the blackness of a beautiful girl's hair, the yellow of the falling leaves, the green of the pine needles, the red, purple, and orange of the flowers around him. All these he put into his bag. As an afterthought, he put the songs of the birds in, too. Then he walked over to the grassy spot where the children were playing. "Children, little children, this is for you," and he gave them his bag. "Open it; there's something nice inside," he told them.

The children opened the bag, and at once hundreds and hundreds of coloured butterflies flew out, dancing around the children's heads, settling on their hair, fluttering up again to sip from this or that flower. The children, enchanted, said that they had never seen anything so beautiful.

The butterflies began to sing, and the children listened smiling.

Just then a songbird came flying, settling on the Creator's shoulder, scolding him, saying: "It's not right to give our songs to these new, pretty things. You told us when you made us that every bird would have his own song and now you've passed them all around. Isn't it enough that you gave your new playthings all the colours of the rainbow?"

"You're right," said the Creator. "I made one song for each bird, and I shouldn't have taken what belongs to you."

So the Creator took the songs away from the butterflies, and that's why they are silent. "They're beautiful even so!" he said.

HOW BUTTERFLIES CAME TO BE: WORKSHEET

Listen to the story, a Native American tale, to find the answers to these questions:

a. What saddened the Creator when he watched the children playing?
b. What did he make the butterflies from?
c. Why did he take the songs away from the butterflies?

Now match the numbers on the left with the letters on the right to find explanations for the new vocabulary:

1. wrinkled		a. began to collect various items
2. blind		b. caused him to feel depressed
3. mangy		c. charmed by what they saw
4. fade		d. criticising
5. made his heart heavy		e. full of lines
6. ground (from to grind)		f. in a bad condition
7. ought to be preserved		g. lose their colour
8. started gathering things		h. made into powder
9. fluttering		i. moving their wings up and down
10. enchanted		j. should be made to last
11. scolding		k. unable to see

"These children will grow old and their skin will become wrinkled. Their hair will turn grey and their teeth will fall out. The young hunter's arm will fail and these lovely young girls will grow fat and ugly". How concerned are you about the signs of ageing? Would you ever consider having cosmetic surgery done? Why or why not? Do you know anybody who has had cosmetic surgery? What were the results like? These are all questions you might like to discuss in small groups. A spokesperson for the group can then be elected to report your findings to the rest of the class.

Why did the Creator make the other creatures that inhabit the Earth? Working in small groups, chose another creature to write a story about. Then choose a spokesperson to tell your story to the rest of the class.

Now match the numbers with the letters to complete these proverbs about animals:

1   A leopard
2   You can lead a horse to water,
3   When the cat's away the mice
4   Barking dogs
5   Birds of a feather
6   Don't count your chickens
7   Don't look a gift horse
8   There's more than one way
9   The early bird
10 Every dog
11 It's no use locking the stable door
12 Let sleeping dogs

a after the horse has bolted.
b before they are hatched.
c but you can't make it drink.
d cannot change its spots.
e catches the worm.
f flock together.
g has his day.
h in the mouth.
i lie.
j seldom bite.
k to skin a cat.
l will play.

WHY THERE ARE MANY LANGUAGES ON EARTH

Level: Intermediate - Advanced

Target Audience: Secondary / Adults

Language / Skills Focus: Listening, Speaking & Writing

Materials: Photocopies of the story (optional) to hand out at the end of the session

IN CLASS

1   There are many ways of learning a language and sitting in a classroom is only one of them. Invite the students to work in small groups to see how many other suggestions they can come up with.

2   An alternative lead-in could be to brainstorm the advantages and disadvantages of establishing a World Language - one language spoken by everyone. The story, which comes from the Philippines, gives a possible explanation as to why there isn't a World Language any more.

3   As a post-listening activity, arrange the students in small groups and invite them to choose one of the following titles to base a story on: *Why People Die /Why Women Have No Beards / Why People Have To Work / Why Men Lose their Hair / Why People Walk On Two Legs*

THE STORY

When the people heard that the rice Dakbungan had planted had come from heaven, some of them wanted to go to heaven too. However, they did not know how Dakbungan got there, so they decided to build a stairway that would take them there.

For many days the people toiled. After a few weeks, the stairway measured taller than a house, but it was still not high enough to reach heaven. After a few months, the stairway was just as high as some of the nearby mountains but still, it could not take the people to heaven.

One day, when the gods looked upon the earth, they saw the stairway and the people busily labouring over it. They said to each other, "Look! The people are trying to reach heaven. This will not do. They're wasting their time. And look at how deserted their villages are. We must put a stop to this."

The gods created lightning and threw the lightning bolts down through the sky. The people at work on the stairway were frightened, for they had never seen lightning bolts before. "Run!" they cried. "What sort of giant spears are these? They seem to be made of fire! The gods must be angry!" In great haste they scrambled down the stairway to seek cover among the bushes and rocks, babbling words they suddenly could not understand. Each of the men had begun to speak a different language.

When all was quiet once more, the men came out of hiding. They had forgotten all about the stairway to heaven, and now they were tired and hungry. One said, "Idawis tako ta styay man-is." Another said, "Ayshi may kekdot et mango say en amis." Another said, "Let's roast our food on a good fire." Still another said, "Saan, ituno tayo tapno naimas."

All of them began to speak at the same time, not knowing that they all meant the same thing. Not being able to understand each other, all of them soon went off to their own villages. As for the stairway, it was never finished since the people no longer spoke in the same tongue.

THE TELLTALE LILAC BUSH

Level: Intermediate – Advanced
Target Audience: Secondary / Adults
Language / Skills Focus: Listening & Role Play / 3rd Conditional
Materials: Photocopies of the worksheet

IN CLASS

Problems between husbands and wives are nothing new. Couples have probably been arguing with each other since the days of Adam and Eve and here's a Hillbilly tale from America that deals with the subject.

After reading the tale, hand out the worksheets. The matching activity is designed to check understanding of the new lexis, the second exercise provides controlled practice in the use of the 3rd conditional, and the third reinforces this by providing the learners with both an opportunity to have some fun with the structure and also to express their creativity. They can then get together in pairs or small groups to compare their alternative endings to the tale.

Match the numbers on the left with the letter on the right to find explanations for the new language in the story: 1-a / 2-i / 3-d / 4-f / 5-h / 6-c / 7-g / 8-b / 9-j / 10-k /11-e

For higher level classes, this stage can be omitted. After reading the tale, you can go straight into the role play.

As a post-listening activity, arrange the students in groups of three for a role play. Student A is the old man pleading his innocence, Student B is the detective carrying out the murder investigation, and Student C is a neighbour who was the old woman's friend.

THE STORY

An old man and woman once lived by themselves on top of a hill by a river. There had been trouble between them for many years and they were always arguing with each other. Few people visited them, and it was not immediately noticed that the wife had unaccountably disappeared.

People suspected that the old man had killed her, but her body could not be found and the question was dropped.

The old man enjoyed life to the full after his wife's disappearance, until one night when a group of young men were sitting on his porch, talking of all the parties the old man was giving. While they were talking, a large lilac bush growing nearby began beating on the window pane and beckoning towards them as if it was trying to tell them something. No one would have thought anything of this if the wind had been blowing. But there was no wind - not even a small breeze.

Paying no attention to the old man's protests, the young men dug up the lilac bush. They were stunned when the roots of the lilac were found to be growing from the palm of a woman's hand.

The old man screamed, ran down the hill towards the river, and was never seen again.

(adapted from a story in *The Second Virago Book of Fairy Tales*, Virago Press Ltd 1992)

THE TELLTALE LILAC BUSH: WORKSHEET

Match the numbers on the left with the letter on the right to find explanations for the new language in the story:

1.	a small breeze	a.	a gentle wind
2.	beckoning	b.	believed to be true
3.	disappeared	c.	cried out in fear
4.	dug up	d.	gone missing
5.	pane	e.	inexplicably
6.	screamed	f.	removed with a spade
7.	stunned	g.	shocked
8.	suspected	h.	sheet of glass
9.	the palm	i.	signalling
10.	the roots	j.	the inside surface of the hand
11.	unaccountably	k.	the underground part of a tree

"No one would have thought anything of this if the wind had been blowing" Retell the story of the old man and woman using the third conditional like the example: The old man and woman were incompatible. They argued a lot. If they hadn't been incompatible, they wouldn't have argued a lot

a. They argued a lot. The old man murdered her.

b. The old man murdered her. He buried her body in the garden.

c. The old woman went missing. People grew suspicious.

d. People grew suspicious. They dug up his garden.

e. They dug up his garden. They found the old woman's body.

f. They found the old woman's body. The old man ran away.

Here is another story that can be retold using the third conditional. However, this time the story is incomplete, and you can choose how you would like it to end. You can do so by adding a maximum of three more third conditional sentences of your own:

1. Romeo got an invitation. He went to a party.
2. He went to a party. He drank too much.
3. He drank too much. He drove dangerously.
4. He drove dangerously. He had an accident.
5. He had an accident. He ended up in hospital.
6. He ended up in hospital. He met a beautiful nurse.
7. He met a beautiful nurse. He fell madly and passionately head over heels in love with her.
8. _____
9. _____
10. _____

Work in groups of three. Student A is the old man pleading his innocence, Student B is the detective carrying out the murder investigation, and Student C is a neighbour who was the old woman's friend.

WHY MOLE LIVES UNDERGROUND

Level: Intermediate - Advanced

Target Audience: Secondary, Adults

Language / Skills Focus: Listening & Writing

IN CLASS

1   While the learners are listening to the Cherokee Indian tale, ask them to find the answers to these questions:

   a. How did the mole help the lovesick man?

   b. What effect did the mole's actions have?

   c. Why has he hid under the ground ever since?

The questions can be boarded before the start of the class or copied on to an OHT

2   After telling the tale, invite the students, working in groups, to write a parallel story choosing one of the following titles: *Why do Zebras have stripes? / Why do Camels have humps? / Why do Bees have stings? / Why do Dalmations have spots? / Why do Giraffes have long necks?*

THE STORY

A man was in love with a woman who disliked him and wanted nothing to do with him. He tried every way he knew how to attract her, but with no success. At last he grew discouraged and made himself sick thinking about it.

Mole came along, and finding the man so depressed, asked him what the trouble was. The man told him the whole story, and when he had finished, Mole said: "I can help you. Not only will she like you by the time I've finished, but she'll come to you of her own free will."

That night, burrowing underground to the place where the girl was in bed asleep, Mole took out her heart. He came back by the same way and gave the heart to the discouraged lover, who couldn't see it even when it was in his hand. "There," said Mole. "Swallow it, and she will be so drawn to you that she will have to come.

The man swallowed the heart, and when the girl woke up she some how thought of him at once. She felt a strange desire to be with him, to go to him that minute. She couldn't understand it because she had always disliked him. But the feeling grew so strong that she was compelled to find the man and tell him that she loved him and wanted to be his wife. And so they were married.

All the magicians who knew them both were surprised and wondered how it had come about. When they found that it was the work of Mole, whom they had always thought too insignificant to notice, they were jealous and threatened to kill him. That's why Mole hid under the ground and has stayed there ever since, only daring to come up to the surface when nobody else is about.

THE HEIGHT OF PURPLE PASSION

Level: Lower Intermediate – Advanced

Target Audience: Secondary / Adults

Language / Skills Focus: Listening, Speaking & Writing, and use of the Indefinite Article to introduce new information

Materials: Photocopies of the worksheet. Photocopies of the story (optional) to hand out at the end of the session.

IN CLASS

1   Start by eliciting what a moral is (a piece of advice that you can learn from a story) Then ask the students to listen to the tale to find an appropriate moral for it. (Curiosity killed the cat perhaps!) They can do this activity in groups and a spokesperson from each group can report back with their conclusions.

2   You might then like to play "I went to a party", which is a variation on the "I went to market" game. This is how it works:

Student A: *I went to a party and I met a lady wearing lipstick.*

Student B; *I went to a party and I met a lady wearing lipstick and a man dressed as a penguin.*

Student C: *I went to a party and I met a lady wearing lipstick, a man dressed as a penguin, and a couple who were deeply in love with each other* (and so on).

The idea is for each member of the class to repeat what the previous person said, and then to add a sentence of their own. The game can be used to provide practice in the use of the indefinite article to introduce new information.

3   Hand out the worksheets, which the learners can work on in pairs.

Match the numbers on the left with the letters on the right to find explanations for the new language in the story: 1-d / 2-c / 3-a / 4-g / 5-f / 6-e / 7-b

Fill in the gaps in the story with these verbs. Use each of the verbs once only: 1. was 2. met 3. did 4. rang 5. flew 6.went 7. told 8. came 9. broke 10. found

4   Arrange the students in small groups and invite them to produce similar stories of their own. Give each group a different proverb to base their story on: *Honesty is the best policy / A bird in the hand is worth two in the bush /Crime doesn't pay / People in glasshouses shouldn't throw stones /Too many cooks spoil the broth / All that glitters is not gold etc., etc.*

5   With higher level classes, elicit what a moral is, narrate the story, and then go on to the final
    stage.

THE STORY

There was this sailor walking down the street and he met a Lady Wearing Lipstick. And she said
to him, 'Do you know what the Height of Purple Passion is?' And he said 'No.' And she said, 'Do
you want to find out?' And he said, 'Yes.' So she told him to come to her house at five o' clock
exactly. So he did, and when he rang the doorbell, birds flew out all around the house. And they
went around the house three times and the door opened and they all flew in again. And there was
the Lady Wearing Lipstick. And she said, 'Do you still want to know what the Height of Purple
Passion is?' And he said he wanted to find out. So she told him to go and take a bath and be very
clean. So he did, and he came running back and slipped on the soap and broke his neck. That's the
end. He never found out what it was. A friend of mine told me this story. It happened to somebody
she knows.

THE HEIGHT OF PURPLE PASSION: WORKSHEET

Match the numbers on the left with the letters on the right to find explanations for the new language in the story:

1. a sailor	a. discover
2. exactly	b. fell
3. find out	c. precisely
4. lipstick	d. someone who works on a ship
5. neck	e. strong feeling
6. passion	f. the part of the body that joins the head to the shoulders
7. slipped	g. what women use to colour their lips

Fill in the gaps in the story with these verbs. Use each of the verbs once only: broke / came / did / flew / found / met / rang / told / was / went

There 1. _____ this sailor walking down the street and he 2. _____ a Lady Wearing Lipstick. And she said to him, 'Do you know what the Height of Purple Passion is?' And he said 'No.' And she said, 'Do you want to find out?' And he said, 'Yes.' So she told him to come to her house at five o' clock exactly. So he 3. _____ , and when he 4. _____ the doorbell, birds 5. _____ out all around the house. And they 6. _____ around the house three times and the door opened and they all flew in again. And there was the Lady Wearing Lipstick. And she said, 'Do you still want to know what the Height of Purple Passion is?' And he said he wanted to find out. So she 7. _____ him to go and take a bath and be very clean. So he did, and he 8. _____ running back and slipped on the soap and 9. _____ his neck. That's the end. He never 10. _____ out what it was. A friend of mine told me this story. It happened to somebody she knows.

Working in small groups, produce similar stories of your own. Each group should take a different proverb to base their story on:

"Honesty is the best policy"
"A bird in the hand is worth two in the bush"
"Crime doesn't pay"
"People in glasshouses shouldn't throw stones"
"Too many cooks spoil the broth"
"All that glitters is not gold" etc etc

Alternatively, or for homework, you might like to use the following opening sentence to start a story with:

There was this _____ walking down the street and he met a _____ Wearing _____ .

THE GYPSY WOMAN AND THE CAVE

Level: Intermediate to Advanced
Target Audience: Secondary, Adults
Language / Skills Focus: Listening & 2nd Conditional
Materials: Photocopies of the story (optional) to hand out at the end of the session

IN CLASS

1   As a pre-listening activity, the learners can work in pairs and take it in turns to find out from each other what their favourite and least favourite months of the year are. The story shows how all the months of the year have qualities to be valued and the dangers of complaining about the weather - however bad it might be!

2   For the while-listening stage, questions inviting the learners to predict what follows next are conveniently built into the text: "They opened it and what do you think they found?" "But when she got back to the city and opened it, what do you think she found?"

3   *Post-Listening:* "And if there were no February, there would be no March" This can be used as a lead-in to work on the 2nd Conditional form. Starting with "If there were no January, there would be no February" you can take the class through all the months of the year. This can be followed by pairwork, in which the learners take it in turns to go through the sequence while being timed by their partners. Who can complete the cycle the quickest!

COMMENTS

At higher levels, stage 3 could be omitted and the story could be used as a springboard into a discussion - on the different ways of predicting the future or the prejudice and persecution that gypsies and other ethnic minorities have to contend with.

THE GYPSY WOMAN AND THE CAVE

Once upon a time, in the old days, Gypsy caravans travelled from village to village, from city to city, and the Gypsies would beg and tell fortunes for a piece of bread.

In one city there was a woman who didn't like her neighbour - the two women were always arguing with each other. This woman called a Gypsy woman over to tell her fortune. "Come here. I'll give you whatever you want if you can tell me what's in my heart."

Just at that moment the neighbour came out of her house and made an insulting gesture to the first woman. The Gypsy noticed this and said, "You live in a really bad neighbourhood and things aren't going well for you in this house. Your neighbours are jealous of you because you're a good housewife and all that."

"Bravo! You found out everything! What do you want me to give you? I'd even give you my heart." So she gave her bread, cheese, and money, and as the Gypsy was leaving for the camp the woman said, "Come tomorrow. I've got something for you to do." The Gypsy promised to return.

At that time Gypsies were forbidden to camp for the night near the city so they had to set up their tents some distance away. The next day, as the Gypsy woman was walking back to the city, all of a sudden it started to rain very hard. It was the month of March. The Gypsy woman searched everywhere for shelter and finally found an entrance to a cave. She went inside and looked around carefully. In the depths of the cave she saw a small light. As she got closer, she saw it was a large fire. "Ah, I'll warm up nicely here."

She looked around and saw twelve young men in nice clothes and good shoes, and they said to her in unison, "Welcome. Tell us, grandmother, where are you going?"

"I'm on my way back to the city, my children, but I got caught in the downpour, and what could I do? I found this cave and came in through the entrance and found you, my golden children."

"Do you know why it's raining? It's the month of March - and in March the cold is awful and the snow ..... what a terrible month it is!"

"Don't say that, my children. The month of March is the best."

"Why?"

"Because it brings us April, when spring comes. Without the month of March, we wouldn't have any spring. And if there were no February, there would be no March."

And so for each of the months she had something good to say.

"And now where are you going?" they asked her.

"I want to return to my tent to feed my hungry children."

"Bring your sack over here," they said, and filled it and sewed it up. "Take it, but don't open it until you get home."

The old woman returned to her tent and said to her children, "Well, today I didn't go to any homes. But I found golden children, little angels, twelve handsome young men. And they gave me this - what is has inside I don't know. Let's see what's inside."

They opened it, and what do you think they found? All golden coins. The twelve young men were really the Twelve months, and the Gypsy woman, because she hadn't insulted any of the months, got the treasure.

The next day the weather was perfectly clear. The Gypsy woman ran to the woman she'd promised to see. As much gold as she'd got, she still wanted to beg - that's the Gypsy way, and that's why people say Gypsies are never satisfied.

On the way she met the quarrelsome neighbour, who recognised her and said, "whatever she gives you, I'll give you more. Now tell me what you want."

"What can I say? I don't want you to give me anything, for God has provided."

"What did God give you?"

So she told her how she'd found the cave and gone in to get out of the rain.

"Where's the entrance to this cave? I'll go and see for myself."

So she went on her way to the Twelve Months but without knowing who they were. She found the entrance just where the Gypsy had told her, and went into the cave, pretending to be cold.

"What month is it, old woman, that it's so cold outside?"

"It's March - the cruellest, worst month in the year."

" And what do you have to say about February?"

"That stupid February?" And she went on to curse all the months, without a good word to say about any of them.

"Give use your sack old woman." They filled it and sewed it up and told her to open it only when she got home. It was so heavy she hoped to find gold inside. She thought it would be the same as the Gypsy's. When she got back to the city and opened it, however, what do you think she found? Lots of snakes that came out and ate everything, including her.

Her neighbour said, "The Gypsy knew everything. My neighbour was truly a bad woman. So the Gypsy did her magic."

That's why since then people, even today, ten million years later, still say that Gypsies know everything, and believe me it's true!

DANCE WITH BOTH HANDS FREE

Level: Upper Intermediate / Advanced

Target Audience: Secondary / Adults

Language / Skills Focus: Listening, Speaking & Writing

Materials: Photocopies of the story (optional) and photocopies of the worksheet

IN CLASS

Pre-listening: Invite the learners to work in pairs, to ask each other the following questions, and then to report back to the rest of the class with their findings:

a. Can stealing ever be justified? If so, when?

b. Have you ever stolen anything and have you been caught? Tell me about it.

c. What can be done to deter shoplifters?

d. What would you do if you discovered that a friend you trusted had stolen something from you?

While-listening: Pause after the line "The weaver went into the kitchen to get a cup of tamarind tea" and ask the students to predict what happened next.

Post-listening: Invite the learners to discuss the following questions in small groups, and then to elect a spokesperson to report back to the rest of the class with their conclusions:

a. Did the weaver have other choices?

b. Did she want her friend to be revealed?

c. What was her intention and why did she take such an approach?

d. And how about the friend? How did she feel? What were her choices?

e. Did the weaver get the thread back?

DANCE WITH BOTH HANDS FREE

Once there was a woman who went to visit her friend. Her friend was a weaver and had been making a beautiful tapestry on her loom. It was woven from beautiful silk threads of many colours. When the weaver saw her friend, she exclaimed; "Friend! I can't tell you how happy I am to see you! What a joyful day. Surely a day for celebration! Please come in and make yourself comfortable, and I'll get you something to drink".

The weaver went into the kitchen to get a cup of tamarind tea. Her friend looked around and noticed the silk threads shimmering in the early afternoon light. They were beautiful and she was tempted. She couldn't resist herself. Quickly, she reached over and took one of the bundles of thread and stuck it underneath her arm.

When the weaver returned she noticed that a bundle of thread was missing, and knew that her friend had taken it. She thought for a moment, and devised a plan to get it back. Putting down the cup of tea she said; "Friend, what a joyful day it is today! Please, get up and let's dance." In a tentative voice her friend responded, "Yes, let us dance".

The weaver raised both her arms high and began to dance. She smiled as she turned in slow circular motions dancing with joy. Her friend got up, but instead danced with both her arms pressed close to her sides, holding the bundle of thread tightly underneath one of her arms. When the weaver saw this she said; "It's a day for celebration friend so why do you dance with your arms that way? Look, dance like me with both your arms raised!" The friend then raised one of her arms, but kept the other pressed tightly against her side. The weaver seeing this insisted and said; "It's such a joyful day, please dance with both arms raised. Look at me. Like this!" The weaver continued to dance, spinning, turning and swaying with joy. The friend looked down and quietly said; "I'm sorry, but this is the only way I know how to dance."

...Always be ready to dance with both hands free

DANCE WITH BOTH HANDS FREE: WORKSHEET

Working in pairs, ask each other the following questions, then report back to the rest of the class with your findings:

a. Can stealing ever be justified, and if so, when?

b. Have you ever stolen anything and have you been caught? Tell me about it.

c. What can be done to deter shoplifters?

d. What would you do if you discovered that a friend you trusted had stolen something from you?

Match the numbers on the left with the letters on the right to find explanations for the new vocabulary.

1.	weaver	a. doing something enjoyable
2.	tapestry	b. felt like doing something forbidden
3.	loom	c. firmly
4.	threads	d. the fruit of a tree grown in warm climates
5.	joyful	e. invented
6.	celebration	f. lifted up
7.	tamarind	g. a machine for making cloth
8.	shimmering	h. moving slowly from one side to another
9.	tempted	i. a person who makes cloth
10.	resist	j. a picture created by sewing threads on to heavy cloth
11.	bundles	k. pieces of cotton
12.	devised	l. refused to accept no as an answer
13.	tentative	m. say no.
14.	tightly	n. shining gently and seeming to move
15.	insisted	o. things tied together
16.	raised	p. turning around quickly
17.	spinning	q. very happy
18.	swaying	r. without confidence

Working in small groups, discuss the following questions. Then elect a spokesperson to report back to the rest of the class:

a. Did the weaver have other choices?

b. Did she want her friend to be revealed?

c. What was her intention and why did she take such an approach?

d. And how about the friend? How did she feel? What were her choices?

e. Did the weaver get the thread back?

THE TWO FROGS

Level: Intermediate – Advanced

Target Audience: Secondary or Adult

Language / Skills Focus: Listening, Speaking & the 3rd conditional

Materials: Photocopies of the worksheet. Photocopies of the story (optional) to hand out to the learners after the session

IN CLASS

1 *Pre-listening:* What do you know about frogs? The story you're going to hear is about two frogs who decide to go on a journey. What do you think they're going to learn from their experiences? Now listen to the story to find out if your predictions are right or not.

2 *Post-listening:* Hand out copies of the worksheet. Here are the answers to the matching activity, the aim of which is to find explanations for the new vocabulary: 1-f / 2-e / 3-l / 4-k / 5-b / 6-h / 7-g / 8-n / 9-d / 10-m / 11-a / 12-c / 13-i / 14-j

3 "If I'd had any idea that Osaka was only a copy of Kyoto I should never have travelled all this way either." Invite the students, working individually, to make sentences of their own like the example, using the frameworks below:

   1. If I'd known (add the name of the place where you are currently studying English) was going to be_____, I'd have_____
   2. If I'd known (add the name of a book you've read) was going to be_____, I'd have_____
   3. If I'd known (add the name of the place where you last went on holiday) was going to be_____, I'd have_____
   4. If I'd known (add the name of a film / play / concert you've been to) was going to be_____, I'd have_____
   5. If I'd known (add the details of a job you've done) was going to be_____, I'd have_____

4 Ask the learners to discuss the questions below in small groups, then to elect a spokesperson to present their views to the rest of the class:

   a. They say that travel broadens the mind. How far do you agree with this statement?
   b. What have you learnt from your travels?
   c. What's the best way to learn about the countries you visit?
   d. What conclusions have you come to about the English based on the experiences you've had?
   e. What advice would you give travellers intending to visit your country?
   f. People are basically the same wherever they come from. How far do you agree with this

statement?

COMMENTS

The Two Frogs, a traditional Japanese tale, comes from *The Violet Fairy Book* by Andrew Lang, Longmans, Green and Co. 1901.

THE TWO FROGS

Once upon a time in Japan there lived two frogs. One made his home in a ditch near the town of Osaka, on the coast, while the other dwelt in a clear little stream which ran through the city of Kyoto. At such a great distance apart, they had never even heard of each other; but, funnily enough, the idea came into both their heads at once that they should like to see a little of the world, and the frog who lived at Kyoto wanted to visit Osaka, and the frog who lived at Osaka wished to go to Kyoto, where the great Mikado had his palace.

So one fine morning in the spring they both set out along the road that led from Kyoto to Osaka, one from one end and the other from the other. The journey was more tiring than they expected because they did not know much about travelling, and halfway between the two towns there was a mountain which had to be climbed. It took them a long time and a great many hops to reach the top, but there were at last, and how surprised they both were when they bumped into one another!

They looked at each other for a moment without speaking, and then fell into conversation, explaining the cause of their meeting so far from their homes. They were delighted to find that they both had the same wish – they both wanted to learn a little more about their native country – as there was no sort of hurry they stretched themselves out in a cool, damp place, and agreed that they would have a little rest before they parted to go their ways.

"What a pity we're not bigger," said the Osaka frog; "for then we could see both towns from here, and tell if it's worth our while going on."

"Oh, that's easily managed," returned the Kyoto frog. "We've only got to stand up on our hind legs, and hold onto each other, and then we can each look at the towns we're travelling to."

This idea pleased the Osaka frog so much that he at once jumped up and put his front paws on the shoulder of his friend, who had also risen. There they both stood, stretching themselves as high as they could, and holding each other tightly, so that they would not fall down. The Kyoto frog turned his nose towards Osaka, and the Osaka frog turned his nose towards Kyoto; but the foolish things forgot that when they stood up their great eyes lay in the backs of their heads, and that though their noses might point to the places where they wanted to go, their eyes beheld the places they had come from.

"Dear me!" cried the Osaka frog, "Kyoto is exactly like Osaka. It's certainly not worth such a long journey. I'm going home!"

"If I'd had any idea that Osaka was only a copy of Kyoto I should never have travelled all this way either," exclaimed the frog from Kyoto, and as he spoke he took his hands from his friend's shoulders, and they both fell down on the grass. Then they both said goodbye to each other and began the long journey home. To the end of their lives they believed that Osaka and Kyoto, which are as different to look at as two towns can be, were as alike as two peas in a pod.

THE TWO FROGS: WORKSHEET

Match the numbers on the left with the letters on the right to find explanations for the new vocabulary.

1.	ditch	a. the back legs of an animal
2.	dwelt	b. jumps
3.	the idea came into both their heads	c. the hands and feet of certain animals
4.	set out	d. left
5.	hops	e. lived
6.	bumped into	f. a long, narrow hole at the side of a road
7.	stretched	g. made their bodies longer and straighter
8.	damp	h. met by chance
9.	parted	i. saw
10.	worth our while	j. similar
11.	hind	k. started (a journey)
12.	paws	l. they both decided
13.	beheld	m. useful for us
14.	alike	n. wet

"If I'd had any idea that Osaka was only a copy of Kyoto I should never have travelled all this way either." Make sentences of your own like the example, using the frameworks below:

1. If I'd known (add the name of the place where you are currently studying English) was going to be_____, I'd have_____
2. If I'd known (add the name of a book you've read) was going to be_____, I'd have_____
3. If I'd known (add the name of the place where you last went on holiday) was going to be_____, I'd have_____
4. If I'd known (add the name of a film / play / concert you've been to) was going to be_____, I'd have_____
5. If I'd known (add the details of a job you've done) was going to be_____, I'd have_____

Working in small groups, discuss the questions below. Then elect a spokesperson to present your views to the rest of the class:

a. They say that travel broadens the mind. How far do you agree with this statement?

b. What have you learnt from your travels?

c. What's the best way to learn about the countries you visit?

d. What conclusions have you come to about the English based on the experiences you have had?

e. What advice would you give travellers intending to visit your country?

f. People are basically the same wherever they come from. How far do you agree with this statement?

THE WISE WOMAN'S STONE

Level: Pre-Intermediate / Intermediate
Target Audience: Adult
Language / Skills Focus: Listening, Speaking & Writing / Tense Revision
Materials: Photocopies of the worksheet

IN CLASS

Pre-listening: What would you do if you were given a precious stone that was worth enough to give you security for a lifetime? Would you keep it or sell it? And if you decided to sell it, what would you do with the money? Now listen to the story to find out what a traveller did when he found himself in this situation.

While-listening: Pause after the line ""I know how valuable this stone is, but I want to give it back to you in the hope that you can give me something even more precious " and ask the listeners to predict what the traveller asks the woman for.

Post-listening: What is the most valuable lesson you've learnt in life that you feel you could pass on to others?

Change the verbs in brackets into the correct tenses, and then complete the last sentence of the tale:
1. was travelling / 2. found / 3. met / 4. was / 5. saw / 6. did / 7. left / 8. knew / 9. was / 10. came / 11. I've been thinking / 12. made

The Ending: ..... what's inside you that others need.

Find words in the story which mean the same as: a. precious / b. a stream / c. wise / d. without hesitation / e. rejoicing in / f. was worth enough / g. security for a lifetime / h. the wealth you have

The Proverbs: 1-g / 2-d / 3-b / 4-j / 5-a / 6-h / 7-c / 8-f / 9-i / 10-e

***

A wise woman who was travelling in the mountains found a precious stone in a stream. The next day she met another traveller who was hungry, and the wise woman opened her bag to share her food. The hungry traveller saw the precious stone and asked the woman to give it to him. She did so without hesitation. The traveller left rejoicing in his good fortune because he knew the stone was worth enough to give him security for a lifetime.

But, a few days later, he came back to return the stone to the wise woman. "I've been thinking," he said. "I know how valuable this stone is, but I want to give it back to you in the hope that you can give me something even more precious. Give me what you have within you that made it possible for you to give me the stone in the first place."

Sometimes it not the wealth you have but what's inside you that others need.

THE WISE WOMAN'S STONE: WORKSHEET

Change the verbs in brackets into the correct tenses, and then complete the last sentence of the tale:

A wise woman who 1. (travel) in the mountains 2. (find) a precious stone in a stream. The next day she 3. (meet) another traveller who 4. (be) hungry, and the wise woman opened her bag to share her food. The hungry traveller 5. (see) the precious stone and asked the woman to give it to him. She 6. (do) so without hesitation. The traveller 7. (leave) rejoicing in his good fortune because he 8. (know) the stone 9 (be) worth enough to give him security for a lifetime. But, a few days later, he 10. (come) back to return the stone to the wise woman. "I 11. (think)," he said. "I know how valuable this stone is, but I want to give it back to you in the hope that you can give me something even more precious. Give me what you have within you that 12. (make) it possible for you to give me the stone in the first place." Sometimes it not the wealth you have but _____.

Find words in the story which mean the same as:

a. extremely valuable
b. a small river
c. clever
d. without stopping to think
e. contented with
f. had sufficient value
g. no more worries for the rest of his days
h. the riches you possess

Have you ever found anything valuable on your travels, or do you know someone else who has? Tell the person sitting next to you about it and / or write about it for homework:

Now match the numbers with the letters to complete these proverbs about travelling:

1. A journey of a thousand miles
2. All roads
3. A rolling stone
4. Bad news
5. Don't burn your bridges
6. Don't cross the bridge
7. If God had meant us to fly, he'd
8. If the mountain won't come to Mohammed
9. It's better to travel hopefully than
10. There's no place

a. behind you.
b. gathers no moss
c. have given us wings.
d. lead to Rome.
e. like home.
f. Mohammed must go to the mountain.
g. starts with a single step.
h. till you come to it.
i. to arrive.
j. travels fast.

THE PEOPLE WHO ALWAYS TALK ABOUT IT

Level: Upper-Intermediate / Advanced
Target Audience: Adult
Language / Skills Focus: Listening & Speaking
Materials: Photocopies of the worksheet. Photocopies of the story (optional).

IN CLASS

Pre-listening: Invite the participants to work in pairs and to ask each other the following questions. They can then report back to the rest of the group with their findings:

a. How important is your job to you?

b. How much time do you spend thinking about it when you're not at work?

c. What's the best / worst aspect of the job you do?

d. How much time do you spend complaining about what you have to do or who you have to work for?

e. How would it affect you if you were made redundant or dismissed? How do you think you'd react to such a situation?

f. What sort of relationship do you have with your colleagues?

Post-Listening: How Assertive are you at Work?

CHECK YOUR SCORE:

a-10 b-5 c-0   6. a-10 b-5 c-0

a-5 b-0 c-10   7. a-0 b-10 c-5

a-5 b-10 c-0   8. a-0 b-5 c-10

a-o b-10 c-5   9. a-10 b-5 c-0

a-5 b-0 c-10   10. a-5 b-10 c-0

WHAT YOUR SCORE MEANS

70-100   You're clearly the kind of person who says what you mean, loud and clear, regardless of the consequences. The problem with being too assertive, however, is that it can make you seem to be unapproachable and inflexible. Remember that listening to others is just as important as making yourself heard.

35-70   You know what you want to say but it doesn't always come out the way you intend it to. You're too concerned about what others will think of you. Remember that being polite and considerate is positive, but so is articulating your own needs and thoughts.

0-35   Saying yes all the time isn't always a good thing – you don't want to be seen as a doormat. Speak up about your achievements and your ambitions. Bosses don't have time to be psychic – learn to be heard and your life will get much easier.

THE PEOPLE WHO ALWAYS TALK ABOUT IT

She was always talking about how much she hated working in the office and about how badly the company was run. In fact, these were the first things she told anyone new who joined. Yet despite her aversion to the place, it was all she ever seemed to talk about. As a result, she got on people's nerves and those in the know avoided her like the plague. Other employees came and went, moved on to better things. Yet she remained behind, and despite all her moaning and groaning, she was the one person you could be certain would be there forever.

At least all of us who knew her thought she'd be. However, one day she went too far and her big mouth landed her in a mess that there was no way out of. The boss caught her telling a new arrival what she thought of him and the company and that was the final straw. He was sick to death of the way she constantly contradicted and tried to belittle him and this was just the excuse he'd been looking for. It was his father who'd initially employed her. However, now that the old man had retired, there was no need to put up with her tiresome behaviour any longer.

What really surprised everyone, however, was not the news of her dismissal but the way she reacted to it. – the weeping and wailing. She literally got down on her knees and begged him to let her stay and to give her another chance. It was distasteful and most embarrassing for the rest of us and we didn't know where to look. I sort of pretended it wasn't happening and just went about my work as usual. It was none of my business and I didn't want to get involved. It turned out that the company was her whole life, especially since her elderly mother had died and she had nothing else to live for. But it was clear that he'd made his decision and there was to be no turning back whatever she did or said.

However, she wouldn't let the matter rest and even took the case to an Industrial Tribunal claiming unfair dismissal. It was a long drawn-out affair as these procedures invariably are. She'd been looking forward to seeing her boss forced to admit he'd been wrong but of course he was represented by a lawyer throughout and so he never even made an appearance at the hearing. She won but it was a hollow victory and the compensation she was paid made little difference to her. She'd had enough money to retire a long time back if that's what she'd really wanted to do.

After that she went downhill fast. It was her neighbours who eventually discovered she was dead when the post started piling up and they noticed the smell coming from her flat. When Social Services broke down the door, they found her seated in her armchair, surrounded by photos taken at the annual office Christmas party. As for the boss, he didn't even bother to attend her funeral. In fact, to be honest, none of us did.

THE PEOPLE WHO ALWAYS TALK ABOUT IT: WORKSHEET

Work in pairs. Ask each other the following questions, and then report back to the rest of the group with your findings:

a.   How important is your job to you?

b.   How much time do you spend thinking about it when you're not at work?

c.   What's the best / worst aspect of the job you do?

d.   How much time do you spend complaining about what you have to do or who you have to work for?

e.   How would it affect you if you were made redundant or dismissed? How do you think you'd react to such a situation?

f.   What sort of relationship do you have with your colleagues?

How Assertive are you at Work?

1.   A colleague asks you to stand in for him at a meeting but you don't have the time. What do you say?
a. Say you'd like to help but you're too busy. b. Ask him if there's anyone else he could ask.
c. Reluctantly agree because you don't feel you can say no.

2.   You're asked for your opinion on something that you feel is a bad idea. What do you do?
a. Point out that while the idea has its advantages, you feel there are also inherent problems.
b. Stutter that you're not absolutely sure about the idea but maybe you haven't quite understood it. c. State clearly you feel it's a bad idea and explain the reasons why.

3.   You've got more work to do than you can manage and your boss asks you how you're coping. How do you react?
a. Tell him you're concerned at how the work is mounting up but you're managing. b. Point out that your workload has become unmanageable and that you need help. c. Say there's a lot of work but you're enjoying the challenge.

4.   Do you make sure you get credit for what you achieve at work?
a. Probably not because you don't like showing off. b. Yes. You make sure people know what you've contributed. c. You prefer to let your achievements speak for themselves.

5.   You're keen to take on more responsibility at work. How do you go about getting it?
a. Grab a couple of minutes in the lift with your boss and let him know. b. Talk to your colleagues about your ambitions but tell your boss you're happy with whatever you get. c. Make an appointment to see your boss to discus the matter.

6. In your appraisal you feel the criticisms made are unjustified. How do you react?
   a. Point out how you feel and explain clearly why. b. Make excuses for your apparent short-comings and agree that you could have been more productive. c. Feel unable to disagree with your boss and accept his opinions.

7. There's an internal promotion going that interests you. Who do you approach?
   a. The boss's secretary to find out if there's a list and put your name on it for consideration.
   b. Everyone involved in the selection procedure to make sure they're aware of your interest.
   c. Briefly mention to your boss that you'd like to be considered.

8. You're behind schedule and need help to meet a deadline. What do you do?
   a. Send an email to some of your colleagues to see if they can help. b. Tell a couple of colleagues you could do with some help if they're not too busy. c. Ask a colleague who owes you a favour and don't take no for an answer.

9. A colleague has pinched an idea of yours and taken all the credit for it. How do you react?
   a. Confront him in front of everyone and insist he tells your boss. b. Tell him how unhappy you are and that you intend to make sure other people know. c. Say nothing to avoid a scene.

10. You're asked to do some overtime over the weekend because there's a crisis on but you've already planned to go away. What do you do?
    a. Explain you've already made other plans and if possible you'd prefer not to come. b. Say straight away that you're going away and there's no way you're coming in. c. Mention you have other plans, but admit they could be cancelled and end up agreeing to work.

THE GYPSY AND THE WOLF

Level: Advanced
Target: Audience: Adults
Language / Skills Focus: Listening, Speaking & Word-building
Materials: Photocopies of the worksheet. Photocopies of the story (optional) to hand out at the end of the session.

IN CLASS

Pre-listening: You have come across the terms communism and capitalism but what other isms can you list? (Fascism, socialism, Catholicism, Judaism, paganism, Buddhism, racism, sexism, consumerism, impressionism, cubism, expressionism) *This story is about ageism.*

While-listening: Pause after the line "It was then he made up his mind" and ask the listeners to predict what the old wolf decided to do next.

Post-listening: Working in small groups, discuss the following questions. Then elect a spokesperson to report back to the rest of the class with your findings:

a.   Which *ism* annoys you most, and why?
b.   How would you define ageism?
c.   Have you been affected or influenced by ageism? Tell me about it?
d.   Are old people in your country respected more or less than in the West?
e.   What can we do on a personal basis to make younger and older members of society feel more valued?
f.   What measures could the Government introduce to put an end to ageism?

"A pack of wolves was led by a sly old beast" We say a group of people but a pack of wolves. Match the numbers on the left with the letters on the right: 1-a/2-j/3-e/4-b/5-i/6-c/7-g/8-d/9-f/10-h

When people are hungry, they wolf down their food. Which other animals can be used as verbs? Fill the gaps in the sentences with the animals listed below. Use each one once only: 1. rat / 2. swans / 3. clam / 4. bugs / 5. badger / 6. worm 7. chicken / 8. carp / 9. crow / 10. grouse / 11. hound / 12. dog

THE GYPSY AND THE WOLF: WORKSHEET

Working in small groups, discuss the following questions. The elect a spokesperson to report back to the rest of the class with your findings:

a. Which *ism* annoys you most, and why?

b. How would you define ageism?

c. Have you been affected or influenced by ageism? Tell me about it?

d. Are old people in your country respected more or less than in the West?

e. What can we do on a personal basis to make younger and older members of society feel more valued?

f. What measures could the Government introduce to put an end to ageism?

"A pack of wolves was led by a sly old beast" We say a group of people but a *pack* of wolves. Match the numbers on the left with the letters on the right:

1.	a colony	a. of ants
2.	a flock	b. of cattle
3.	a gaggle	c. of dolphins
4.	a herd	d. of fish
5.	a litter	e. of geese
6.	a pod	f. of insects
7.	a pride	g. of lions
8.	a school	h. of monkeys
9.	a swarm	i. of puppies
10.	a troop	j. of sheep

When people are hungry, they *wolf* down their food. Which other animals can be used as verbs? Fill the gaps in the sentences with the animals listed below. Use each one once only: badger / bugs / carp / chicken / clam / crow / dog / grouse / hound / rat / swans / worm

1. How could you _____on your very best friend like that? You should be ashamed of yourself!
2. He_____around the office as if he owns the place but in fact he's just a clerk.
3. Some people explode when they're angry whereas others just _____up.
4. The way she keeps contradicting what I say really_____me.
5. Don't_____me to lend you money. Go out and find a job!
6. You can't_____your way into my affections so you might as well give up!
7. When the crunch came to the crunch, I thought he'd_____out of a confrontation and he proved me right.
8. I wish she wouldn't_____on about her illnesses all the time. I find it really depressing.
9. Stop being so big-headed! Considering you won the match against an injured opponent, you've really got nothing at all to _____ about.
10. Foreign visitors to England tend to_____about the food and the weather. They also complain about how unfriendly the English people are.
11. If the press keeps publishing scandalous stories about the President's private life, they could_____him out of office.
12. She's had one illness after another. Bad health seems to _____her and she's really been very unlucky.

THE GYPSY AND THE WOLF

A pack of wolves was led by a sly old beast who had seen many dangers in his long life. He had spat in death's eye many a time, yet emerged triumphant from all his fights.

The old wolf knew the forest laws, knew the forest did not spare the weak, and knew also that one day he would be too old to lead the pack. Then they would not spare him.

Though his old wounds prevented him from hunting as well as in his younger days, he still got by with cunning, and always ran on ahead to seek out the prey.

But one cold winter the hunting was lean and for the first time he saw hatred and contempt in the pack's grey eyes. No longer were young wolves afraid of him because they knew he was getting old. The entire pack had patiently waited this moment when it could turn on its once-strong leader.

It was then he made up his mind.

Waiting till deepest night, the old wolf rose silently and started to slink away, distancing himself from the hungry wolves. But they sensed his flight and took up pursuit, though they were not as wise in forest lore as he was. He kept just ahead of them, making for a clearing where he knew a lone gypsy's cottage stood.

At one time that gypsy, too, had been leader of a pack. And what a mighty gypsy pack it had been! He had led his gypsies down many tracks, had been wise and bold, and his word had often saved the pack from misfortune.

The time came, however, when old age withered the leader's strength, he could feel it in his bones. He was not strong enough to hold the reins or to keep young braves in check any more.

One time, when the clan was wintering in a village and the gypsy families were quartered in huts, the old chief summoned up his remaining strength and stole away to build himself a cottage in the forest. And that spring, when the gypsy band moved off, the chief was not with them; he remained alone in the forest. No one had seen him. He must have fallen victim to hungry wolves or vanished into a snowdrift.

He did run into wolves, true enough. Yet though he was quite unarmed, the wolf pack did not touch him because their leader had forbidden it. The old man knew not why.

So the gypsy lived alone in the middle of the forest. He feared no one and when one night he heard an eerie wolf cry near his hut, he lit a torch and opened the door. The yellow-flecked grey eyes of the old wolf stared up at him, as if he was asking for aid. At the margin of the trees, he could see the wolf pack waiting to attack. But as he swung his torch, the wolves slunk back, merging with the gloom.

The two old-timers, the gypsy and the wolf, looked fondly at each other. And the gypsy patted the old leader's furry head as he lay meekly at his feet.

WILLOW WIFE

Level: Advanced
Target Audience: Adult
Language / Skills Focus: Listening & Speaking / Tree Idioms
Materials: Photocopies of the worksheet

IN CLASS

Pre-listening: You could start with a brainstorming session by asking what we depend on trees for. Alternatively, you might like to ask the learners to consider the following question: *If you could choose a tree to be your partner, what kind of tree would you choose, and why?*

Post-Listening: Hand out copies of the worksheet.

Match the numbers on the left with the letters on the right to find explanations for the new vocabulary: 1-g / 2-h / 3-a / 4-b / 5-e / 6-I / 7-j / 8-c / 9-d / 10-f

Working in small groups, discuss the following questions. Elect a spokesperson to take notes and to present your views to the rest of the class:

  a. Some people believe in talking talk to their plants. Have you ever spoken to a tree or a plant? Tell me about it.
  b. Do you think plants and trees have feelings in the same way that people do?
  c. Why are trees so important for our survival?
  e. What do you do on a personal level to stop trees being cut down unnecessarily and to care for the environment?
  f. What other myths or legends do you know about trees?

Complete the idioms with the words listed. You may need some of the words more than once and some not at all! 1. woods / 2. trees / 3. branch / 4. root / 5. tree / 6. leaf / 7. trees / 8. leaf / 9. roots / 10. stick

COMMENTS

This traditional Japanese tale is an adaptation of a story in *Myths and Legends of Japan* by F. Hadland Davis, published by G. G. Harrap and Company in 1913.

WILLOW WIFE: WORKSHEET

Match the numbers on the left with the letters on the right to find explanations for the new vocabulary:

1.	imposing	a. a hole in the ground for a corpse
2.	timber	b. a look that lights up the world
3.	a grave	c. a sound that cuts through the silence like a knife
4.	radiant smile	d. cried bitterly
5.	in due time	e. eventually
6.	ineffectual	f. showing signs of great pain
7.	couldn't have borne	g. something that makes a big impression on you
8.	piercing cry	h. wood used for building
9.	sobbed	i. words that makes no difference
10.	agonized	j. would have been unable to put up with

Working in small groups, discuss the following questions. Elect a spokesperson to take notes and to present your views to the rest of the class:

a. Some people believe in talking talk to their plants. Have you ever spoken to a tree or a plant? Tell me about it.

b. Do you think plants and trees have feelings in the same way that people do?

c. Why are trees so important for our survival?

e. What do you do on a personal level to stop trees being cut down unnecessarily and to care for the environment?

f. What other myths or legends do you know about trees?

Complete the idioms with the words listed. You may need some of the words more than once and some not at all!

branch / forest / leaf / root / roots / stick / tree / trees / twigs / woods /

1. The patient's made a partial recovery but is still not out of the _____ yet.
2. The situation's much more complicated than I realised and it's difficult to see the wood for the _____.
3. You're an adult now and you can't live at home with your parents forever. The time has come to _____ out and to make a new life for yourself.
4. They say that money is the _____ of all evil but, in my opinion, it depends on what you do with it.
5. You're wrong to suggest I was to blame for what happened. The truth is you're barking up the wrong _____.
6. You're shaking like a _____. What on earth's the matter with you?
7. Money doesn't grow on _____ and you really need to make an effort to be more economical.
8. The time has come to make a fresh start and to turn over a new _____.
9. You can't remain on your own forever. It's time you got married and put down _____ somewhere.
10. It's clear you don't understand what's happened because you seem to have got hold of the wrong end of the _____.

WILLOW WIFE

In a certain Japanese village there grew a great willow tree. For many generations the people loved it. In the summer it was a resting place, a place where the villagers might meet after the work and heat of the day were over, and there talk till the moonlight streamed through the branches. In winter it was like a great half-opened umbrella covered with sparkling snow.

Heitaro, a young farmer, lived quite near this tree, and the imposing willow was very important to him. It was almost the first object he saw when he woke up each day, and when he returned from work in the fields he looked out eagerly for its familiar form. Sometimes he would kneel down and pray beneath its branches. One day an old man of the village came to Heitaro and explained to him that the villagers were anxious to build a bridge over the river, and that they wanted the tree for timber.

"For timber?" said Heitaro, hiding his face in his hands. "My dear willow tree for a bridge? Never, never, old man!" When Heitaro had somewhat recovered himself, he offered to give the old man some of his own trees instead if he and the villagers would spare the ancient willow.

The old man readily accepted this offer, and the willow tree continued to stand in the village as it had stood for so many years.

One night while Heitaro sat under the great willow he suddenly saw a beautiful woman standing close beside him, looking at him shyly, as if she wanted to speak.

"Honourable lady," he said, "I'll go home now. I can see you're waiting for someone. Heitaro is not without kindness towards those who love."

"He won't come now," said the woman, smiling.

"Can he have grown cold? How terrible it is when a false love comes and leaves ashes and a grave behind!"

"He hasn't grown cold, dear lord."

"And yet he doesn't come! What strange mystery is this?"

"He has come! His heart's always been here, here under this willow tree." And with a radiant smile the woman disappeared.

Night after night they met under the old willow tree. The woman's shyness had entirely disappeared, and it seemed that she could not hear too much from Heitaro's lips in praise of the willow where they sat.

One night he said to her, "Little one, will you be my wife — you who seem to come from the very tree itself?"

"Yes," said the woman. "Call me Higo ("Willow") and, if you love me, ask no questions. I've got no father or mother, and someday perhaps you'll understand."

Heitaro and Higo got married. In due time they were blessed with a child whom they called Chiyodo, and they were the happiest people in all Japan.

One day great news came to the village. The villagers were full of it, and it was not long before it reached Heitaro's ears. The ex-Emperor Toba wished to build a temple to Kwannon [The Goddess of Mercy] in Kyoto, and those in authority sent far and wide for timber. The villagers decided that they must contribute towards the building by presenting their great willow tree. Heitaro's promise of other trees was ineffectual this time because neither he nor anyone else could give such a large and handsome tree as the great willow.

Heitaro went home and told his wife the dreadful news. Before I married you I couldn't have borne it," he said. But having you, little one, perhaps I'll get over it someday."

That night Heitaro was woken up by a piercing cry.

"Heitaro," said his wife, "it grows dark! The room is full of whispers. Are you there, Heitaro? Listen! They're cutting down the willow tree. Look how its shadow trembles in the moonlight. I'm the soul of the willow tree. The villagers are killing me. They're tearing me to pieces! The pain, the pain!

"My Willow Wife! My Willow Wife!" sobbed Heitaro.

"Husband," said Higo, very faintly, pressing her wet, agonized face close to his, "I'm going now. But a love like ours can never be cut down, however fierce the blows, and I'll be waiting for you and Chiyodo on the other side. My hair's falling through the sky! My body's breaking!"

There was a loud crash outside. The great willow tree lay cut down on the ground. Heitaro looked round for the one he loved more than anything else in the world. Willow Wife had gone!

THE BALD-HEADED MAN

Level: Intermediate
Target Audience: Adults
Language / Skills Focus: Listening & Speaking
Materials: Photocopies of the worksheets

IN CLASS

Pre-listening: If you believed you were possessed by evil spirits, who would you turn to for help? Now read / listen to the story to find out what the man in the story did.

While-listening: Pause after the words 'The god says if a man is bald-headed .....' and ask the listeners to predict what follows.

Post-listening: Put the ten parts of the story in the correct order: 1-b 2-d 3-a 4-g 5-h 6-I 7-j 8-e 9-f 10-c

Match the numbers on the left with the letters on the right to find explanations for the new vocabulary: 1-j 2-i 3-b 4-g 5-e 6-a 7-k 8-f 9-h 10-d 11-c

Working in small groups, discuss the following questions. Elect a spokesperson to take notes and to present your views to the rest of the class:

a. If you found you were losing your hair, what would you do about it?
b. How would you feel about having a hair transplant?
c. What else would you like to change about your appearance, and why?
d. Do you know anyone who has had cosmetic surgery? Tell me about it
e. Would you ever consider having cosmetic surgery? Why or why not?

COMMENTS

The Bald-Headed Man has been adapted from a story in "Tibetan Folk Tales" translated by A. L. Shelton, M.D., edited by Flora Beal Shelton (New York: George H. Doran Company, 1925)

THE BALD HEADED MAN

A long time ago, when the world was young and men and women were ill because an evil spirit possessed them, there lived a man and his wife who were very poor. A devil came and took possession of each of them and made them both sick. As they were not rich they couldn't invite a holy man to read prayers for them, so they invited someone else instead, a friend of a friend who was said to know a lot about such things.

After a while this man who was reading began to get very hungry. It was the custom to give the priests the best of food, but this man and his wife had no fine things to eat. They had no horses, no yak and only one goat. So the reader began to think to himself that if they would kill this goat he'd have plenty to eat, as it was really pretty fat.

The man who owned the house was bald-headed and now he came up and sat on the roof near where the man was reading. He sat down in front of him and heard the man mumbling his prayers, "Om mani padme hum. Om mani padme hum," he was reading, and read right on in the same tone, "The god says if a man is bald-headed and will take the skin of a goat and put it on his head he will have hair."

The old man sat and heard him read this over several times and finally decided it was there in the book of prayers; so he killed the goat.

They all had some good eating for a while, and the old man put the skin on his head, wore it and wore it for days and days and kept feeling his head, but not a single hair would come. He finally concluded that the man had lied to him out of the book, and besides, he thought, "If I wear this too long, I fear all the skin will be worn off my head and there will be nothing but bone."

So he asked the man about it, whether he hadn't lied to him, and he said, "O, no, but if a man would have what the gods say come true, he must pray a great deal himself." And that's how he managed to get away with his lies and had goat to eat as well.

THE BALD-HEADED MAN: WORKSHEET (i)

Place the ten parts of the story in the correct order:

a. After a while this man who was reading began to get very hungry. It was the custom to give the priests the best of food, but this man and his wife had no fine things to eat. They had no horses, no yak and only one goat.

b. A long time ago, when the world was young and men and women were ill because an evil spirit possessed them, there lived a man and his wife who were very poor. A devil came and took possession of each of them and made them both sick.

c. And that's how he managed to get away with his lies and had goat to eat as well.

d. As they were not rich they couldn't invite a holy man to read prayers for them, so they invited someone else instead, a friend of a friend who was said to know a lot about such things.

e. He finally concluded that the man had lied to him out of the book, and besides, he thought, "If I wear this too long, I fear all the skin will be worn off my head and there will be nothing but bone."

f. So he asked the man about it, whether he hadn't lied to him, and he said, "O, no, but if a man would have what the gods say come true, he must pray a great deal himself."

g. So the reader began to think to himself that if they would kill this goat he'd have plenty to eat, as it was really pretty fat.

h. The man who owned the house was bald-headed and now he came up and sat on the roof near where the man was reading. He sat down in front of him and heard the man mumbling his prayers, "Om mani padme hum. Om mani padme hum," he was reading, and read right on in the same tone, "The god says if a man is bald-headed and will take the skin of a goat and put it on his head he will have hair."

i. The old man sat and heard him read this over several times and finally decided it was there in the book of prayers; so he killed the goat.

j. They all had some good eating for a while, and the old man put the skin on his head, wore it and wore it for days and days and kept feeling his head, but not a single hair would come.

ANSWERS: 1 _____ 2 _____ 3 _____ 4 _____ 5 _____ 6 _____ 7 _____ 8 _____ 9 _____ 10_____

THE BALD-HEADED MAN: WORKSHEET (ii)

Match the numbers on the left with the letters on the right to find explanations for the new vocabulary:

1.	holy	a.	an animal with horns that is kept for the milk it produces
2.	evil spirits	b.	controlled
3.	possessed	c.	escape without being punished
4.	devil	d.	in any case
5.	yak	e.	a silky-haired animal found in Tibet
6.	goat	f.	speaking too quietly and not clear enough to be understood
7.	bald	g.	the most powerful evil spirit, said to live in Hell
8.	mumbling	h.	the words you say to God
9.	prayers	i.	very bad beings
10.	besides	j.	very religious
11.	get away with	k.	without any hair

Working in small groups, discuss the following questions. Elect a spokesperson to take notes and to present your views to the rest of the class:

a. If you found you were losing your hair, what would you do about it?

b. How would you feel about having a hair transplant?

c. What else would you like to change about your appearance, and why?

d. Do you know anyone who has had cosmetic surgery? Tell me about it.

e. Would you ever consider having cosmetic surgery? Why or why not?

THE OUTCAST

Level: Upper-Intermediate / Advanced
Target Audience: Adult
Language / Skills Focus: Listening & Speaking
Materials: Photocopies of the worksheet

IN CLASS

Pre-listening: What would you do if your family didn't approve of the person you loved? Would you end the relationship to respect their wishes or would you defy them? That's what the story that follows is all about.

As an alternative to the above activity, you might like to use the following: *An outcast is someone who has been rejected by society. What reasons could there be for something like this happening? Working in small groups, make a list of the possible causes. … Now listen to find out if the man in the story became an outcast for one of the reasons you listed.*

While-listening: Pause after the words "If that's the way he feels …" and ask the listeners to predict how the chieftain responded to the gypsy's show of defiance.

Pause after the words "Finally the old man broke the silence" and ask the students to predict what the old man said.

Post-listening: What would you have done if you'd been the gypsy and you'd been abandoned by your tribe? Would you have followed them or would you have followed your own path? Have you ever found yourself in a similar predicament to this? If so, how did you react?

Hand out copies of the worksheet. The learners can work through the questionnaires individually, marking the statement for each question that correspond best to how they feel. They can then be invited to form groups where they can read the interpretations of their scores to the other members, from whom they can receive feedback. In other words, do the members of the group agree or disagree with the analysis?

CHECK YOUR SCORE:

1. a-2 b-4 c-6 / 2. a-6 b-4 c-7 d-2 e-1 / 3. a-4 b-2 c-5 d-7 e-6 / 4. a-4 b-6 c-2 d-1 / 5. a-6 b-4 c-3 d-5 e-2 / 6. a-6 b-4 c-2 / 7. a-6 b-2 c-4 / 8. a-6 b-7 c-5 d-4 e-3 f-2 g-1 / 9. a-7 b-6 c-4 d-2 e-1 / 10. a-4 b-2 c-3 d-5 e-6 f-1

THE OUTCAST

Down through the ages the meeting of gypsy tribes has not always been friendly as they have long been hostile to one another.

One upon a time a gypsy from the Lovary tribe fell in love with a girl from the Servo clan. What could he do? He was determined to marry her, but how could he go against the gypsy word? Finally, he went to tell his problems to the chieftain, but the old man would not listen.

"You can't go against gypsy law," was all he said.

"To hell with the law that spoils our happiness," retorted the gypsy angrily.

That set the whole camp muttering against him.

"How dare he spit on gypsy law!"

"It's a wonder the earth doesn't strike him down dead!"

"If that's the way he feels," said the gypsy chieftain, holding up his hand for silence, "we don't need him any more. Let him learn what it's like to be on his own."

The chieftain then instructed the gypsies to gather up their things and take to the road, abandoning the hot-headed gypsy.

Once alone, the gypsy felt lost and confused. He glanced from the whip tightly clenched in his hand to the branches above. Then he sank to his knees to blow on the dying embers of the fire but the fire had no will to live. After a while the gypsy grew afraid and ran in pursuit of the departing tribe. He ran in panic, his lungs bursting, often tripping over and full of dread, pulling himself up and rushing on. He stuck fast to the narrow rut made by the gypsy wagons.

Only at dawn, as he reached a riverbank, did he see his gypsy band at rest. Beside a tent on the high river bank by a fading fire sat an old man, smoking a pipe.

"Old man," cried the outcast, "was the chieftain right to drive me out for love? Is it my fault the girl and I are from different tribes?"

The old fellow remained silent. He did not even glance towards the gypsy, just continued puffing on his pipe and staring into the embers.

In his anger the young gypsy began to curse the world – the chieftain for driving him out, the gypsy girl who could not be his, and the gypsies for their unfair laws.

"Old man, surely you know I'm right," he cried. "You're just scared of going against gypsy law."

Finally the old man broke his silence. "You broke gypsy law three times. You cursed your brothers who nurtured you, you cursed the fire that warmed you, and you cursed the one you love. Aren't you worthy of your punishment?"

"You can't punish a man for love!"

"You're not being punished for love, but for hate."

"Hate ..." the old man quietly repeated. Just then, in the moonlight, a knife flashed and entered the heart of the headstrong gypsy.

THE OUTCAST: WORKSHEET

An outcast is seen as someone who has been rejected by society and does not fit in. How do other people see you? Complete the following questionnaire to find out!

1. When do you feel at your best?
   a. early in the morning b. during the afternoon and early evening c. late at night

2. How would you describe the way you walk?
   a. fairly fast with long steps b. fairly fast with short quick steps c. not very fast, head up
   d. not very fast, head down e. very slowly

3. How do you stand when talking to people?
   a. with your arms folded b. with your hands clasped c. with your hands on your hips
   d. you touch the person you're talking to
   e. you play with your ear, touch your chin or smooth your hair

4. When you're relaxing, how do you sit?
   a. with your knees bent and your legs side by side b. with your legs crossed
   c. with your legs stretched out d. with one leg curled under you

5. How do you react when something amuses you?
   a. with a big appreciative laugh b. with a laugh but not a loud one
   c. with a quiet chuckle d. with a sheepish smile

6. How do you behave at parties?
   a. make a loud entrance so everyone notices you
   b. make a quiet entrance, looking around for someone you know
   c. try to stay unnoticed

7. If you're interrupted while you're working, how do you react?
   a. a. welcome the break b. feel extremely irritated c. vary between these extremes

8. Which of the following colours do you like the most?
   a. red or orange b. black c. yellow or light blue d. green e. dark blue or purple f. white

9. How do you lie in bed before going to sleep?
   a. on your back b. on your stomach c. on your side
   d. with your head on one arm e. with your head under covers

10. What do you tend to dream about?

a. falling b. fighting or struggling c. searching for something or someone

d. flying or floating e. you usually have a dreamless sleep f. your dreams are always pleasant

WHAT YOUR SCORE MEANS:

60+   Others see you as someone they should handle with care. You're seen as vain, self-centred and extremely dominant. They may wish they could be more like you but they don't trust you and they hesitate to become too deeply involved.

51-60   Your friends consider you to be exciting, highly volatile and rather impulsive. They see you as being a natural leader and quick to make decisions, although not always the right ones. They regard you as someone who will try anything once and someone who is prepared to take a chance. They enjoy being in your company because of the excitement you radiate.

41-50   Other people see you as lively, charming, practical and always interesting, someone who is always the centre of attention but not big-headed about it. They also know you to be kind and considerate, someone who will cheer them up and help them out.

31-40   Others see you as sensible, cautious and practical. Not a person who makes friends easily, but someone who is extremely loyal to the friends you do make and who expects the same loyalty in return

21-30   Friends see you as a fussy, slow and stately plodder. It would really surprise them if you ever did something impulsive. They expect you to examine everything carefully from every possible angle and then, usually, to decide against it.

11-20   People think you are shy, nervous and indecisive, someone who needs to be looked after, who always wants someone else to make the decisions and who doesn't want to get involved with anyone or anything. They see you as a worrier who invents problems that don't really exist.

THE CLOCK

Level: Upper Intermediate /Advanced
Target Audience: Adults
Language / Skills Focus: Listening & Speaking
Materials: Photocopies of the worksheets to hand out after the storytelling

IN CLASS

Pre-listening: The story you're going to hear is about a clock. What sort of clock do you suppose it is and what's special about it? Now read or listen to the tale to find out whether your predictions were accurate or not.

Post-listening: Hand out copies of Worksheet 1. The learners can work individually on the matching activity, and can then be invited to get together in groups to compare their answers. This way you cater for both intrapersonal and interpersonal intelligence types and nobody gets frustrated with the process. Then invite someone to the front of the room to board their answers, which the rest of the class can check to see whether they agree or not.

Without looking back at the text, if possible, match the numbers with the letters like the example: 1-h / 2-a / 3-e / 4-b / 5-i / 6-j / 7-l / 8-g / 9-k / 10-c / 11-d / 12-f

For Worksheet 2, ask the learners to work together in small groups. Give the questionnaire to one person only in the group. The student with the questionnaire is the interviewer. He / she presents the questionnaire to the group as a listening comprehension activity. Encourage this person to take on the role of the teacher, explaining or simplifying the questions as required, while the group members make a note of their answers individually. Then hand out copies of the worksheets to everyone in the room so they can check their scores, read about what the scores mean, and then discuss whether they agree with the interpretations offered or not.

On Worksheet 3 the focus is on proverbs connected with time, with both a matching activity and then freer practice that entails writing dialogues.

Match the numbers with the letters to complete these proverbs about time: 1-i / 2-k / 3-p / 4-f / 5-m / 6-a / 7-l / 8-c / 9-b / 10-g / 11-j / 12-h / 13-d / 14-n / 15-o / 16-e

At the end of the lesson, the following assignment could be set for homework: Describe a special object of yours, and why it is important to you.

THE CLOCK

It had been his grandfather's – a battered old travelling alarm-clock that had to be wound up every twenty four hours and always lost time, a regular ten minutes a day. And although modern replacements were available cheaply that were clearly much more convenient to operate, there was no way he could bring himself to part with it. The clock was the one possession his grandfather had left him that Daniel felt he could make use of and that's why, despite its obvious limitations, he chose to hang on to it.

So whatever time he set the clock for, the bell would ring ten minutes earlier. The problem was exacerbated by his own in-built clock, which conditioned him to wake up ten minutes before the bell actually went off. However, this suited Daniel just fine as he had a fixation with time.

Daniel had an answer for just about everything except the one question he always dreaded – when people asked him if he was happy. How can anyone truly say they're happy given the state the world is in? This would be his stock reply. However, in reality, the concept of happiness was beyond his comprehension. For Daniel's only concern in life was not to waste any precious time and nothing else really mattered.

Being a born worrier, he was in constant fear of being late and not making the most of the time he had. Even at weekends he could never manage to lie in like other people seemed to do. On Friday nights, to please his long-suffering wife, he would break his weekday habit of setting the clock. However, he knew that only too well, his in-built clock would never fail him and that he would still wake up the same time as usual.

In reality, the policy was counter-productive as most of the time he was so overtired that he was unable to produce any work of value or to appreciate the extra time that he did have. In fact, the problem got worse and worse, until eventually his nerves became totally frayed and it was apparent to all around him, and even Daniel himself, that he was in desperate need of help.

That's when the clock decided to take over. One morning despite the usual preparations Daniel had made to wind up the clock and set the alarm the night before, it chose not to go off. Moreover, his in-built clock chose not to operate too. It was as if the two clocks were in league with each other. And so Daniel slept blissfully on until lunchtime. And instead of waking up guilt-ridden and in a panic, he woke up refreshed and revitalized.

As far as Daniel was concerned, it was the first morning of spring. And the first thing he did once he'd got dressed was to go outside into the garden and to dig a hole. There he buried the clock, which had served its purpose, and from that moment on he never looked back. For Daniel had rediscovered his birthright - how to truly enjoy the life he'd been blessed with. And, from that day on, Daniel had no trouble answering the question that had previously so perplexed him. For the sound of the ticking that had so plagued him had finally stopped.

THE CLOCK: WORKSHEET 1

Without looking back at the text, if possible, match the numbers with the letters like the example.

Example: **1-h**

1. **battered**
2. much more convenient to operate
3. part with it
4. despite its obvious limitations
5. hang on to it
6. exacerbated
7. had a fixation with
8. beyond his comprehension
9. lie in
10. in league with each other
11. guilt-ridden
12. plagued him

a. a lot easier to use
b. although it was far from perfect
c. collaborating
d. feeling he'd done something wrong
e. get rid of it
f. got on his nerves
g. impossible for him to understand
h. **in a poor state of repair**
i. keep it
j. made worse
k. stay in bed late
l. was obsessed with

Work in pairs. Ask each other the following questions and then report back to the rest of the class with you findings:

a. What time do you usually turn up for appointments – on time, early, or late?
b. If you were meeting someone on a date, how long would you be prepared to wait for them if they were late?
c. What would you do about an employee who kept turning up late for work?
d. Are you an early riser or do you tend to lie in whenever you get the chance?
e. How much importance do you attach to time – too much or too little?

THE CLOCK: WORKSHEET 2

How stressed out are you?

1. How do you react when something upsets you or winds you up?
   a. You think about it for a day or two.
   b. You can't get it out of your head for a week or more.
   c. Your thoughts quickly turn to other things.

1. How do you feel when you think about all the jobs you have to do during the day?
   a. You usually feel you can cope well despite the pressures.
   b. You feel wound up but expect to get through it.
   c. You feel overwhelmed and think you'll never be able to do them.

1. How does your body feel on a typical day?
   a. Tense across the neck and shoulders.
   b. Relaxed. Your breathing is always easy and slow.
   c. Very stiff in the neck and shoulders and you're prone to frequent headaches.

1. How do you react to the situations you find yourself in feel during the course of an average day?
   a. You tend to lose your temper over unimportant things.
   b. You get more irritated by things going wrong then you would like.
   c. You cope calmly with life's usual setbacks.

1. What's your sleeping pattern like?
   a. You have no problems sleeping.
   b. You wake up frequently during the night and often feel tired the next day.
   c. You get odd nights of bad sleep but can usually make up for them.

1. How do you react when you think of what other people expect from you in life?
   a. You panic and feel inadequate.
   b. You can keep a sense of perspective. You know there are lots of things you can't do, and that's fine.
   c. You take their opinions seriously but you don't lose any sleep over them.

CHECK YOUR SCORES:

1	a-2 b-3 c-1	2	a-1 b-2 c-3	3	a-2 b-1 c-3
4	a-3 b-2 c-1	5	a-1 b-3 c-2	6	a-3 b-1 c-2

WHAT YOUR SCORE MEANS:

11 – 18: You clearly feel stressed out and need to do something about it. Make sure you do some regular exercise or take up meditation or yoga. Reduce your intake of stimulants such as nicotine and caffeine. Eat non-fatty, wholesome starchy foods and avoid sugars. And, most important of all, learn how to say no.

10 – 14: Your stress levels are about average, but you should do what you can to lower them so read the tips above.

6 – 9: You're doing well and have nothing to worry about. We live in a stressful world but it's obvious you can cope. You can set a good example for those around you to follow so they can learn how to keep their stress levels under control too.

THE CLOCK: WORKSHEET 3

Match the numbers with the letters to complete these proverbs about time:

1	Better late than	a	a great healer.
2	A stitch in time	b	at forty.
3	Good things come to those	c	every minute.
4	The darkest hour is	d	in a day.
5	Time and tide	e	is hot.
6	Time is	f	just before the dawn.
7	There's no time like	g	knocks once .
8	There's one born	h	less speed.
9	Life begins	i	never.
10	Opportunity only	j	never comes.
11	Live for today for tomorrow	k	saves nine.
12	More haste,	l	the present.
13	Rome wasn't built	m	wait for no man.
14	Never put off until tomorrow	n	what you can do today.
15	Make hay	o	while the sun shines.
16	Strike while the iron	p	who wait.

Now, working with a partner, write a dialogue incorporating as many of the proverbs as you can. When you are ready, you will be asked to read the dialogue out to the rest of the class and they will listen to count up how many you have used and to make sure you have used them correctly. The couple who manage to use the most proverbs will be awarded a fabulous mystery prize!

PARTS OF THE BODY

Level: Pre-Intermediate / Intermediate

Target Audience: Younger Learners or Adults

Language / Skills Focus: Listening & Speaking

Materials: Photocopies of the worksheets to hand out after the storytelling

IN CLASS

Pre-listening: As a lead-in to the story, you could start with an alphabet game. The aim is for each student to repeat the previous student's list and add a body part of their own, starting with the next letter of the alphabet!

I've got an arm.

I've got an arm and a bottom.

I've got an arm, a bottom and a chest.

I've got an arm, a bottom, a chest and some digits etc.

Possible answers: eyes / feet / gall bladder / hair or hips / index finger / jaw / knees / legs / mouth / nose / ovaries or organs of speech / pores or a palate / a quaff or a quirk / ribs or retinas / shoulders or shins / toes or thighs / unmentionable parts / varicose veins / wrist or a waist / x-ray vision / zap or a zit

Write the following words on pieces of paper and give them out to the learners before they listen to the text: limbs / body / arms / legs / stomach / feet / hands / eyes / ears / nose / tongue. Tell the class you're going to read a story to them and every time they hear the word that is written on their slip of paper, they stand up and sit down again. This activity is ideal for the kinesthetic learners as it gives them an opportunity to stretch their legs and listening for the words to come up in the story helps to hold the learners' attention during the while-listening stage.

Post-listening: Hand out the worksheets for the gap fill activity for the learners to decide on a moral to the tale and to complete the gap fill activity.

Complete the story by putting the missing words below into the gaps: 1. limbs 2. complained 3. sick 4. paying 5. strike 6. refused 7. avoided 8. deaf 9. taste 10. upset 11. situations 12. lay 13. because 14. lost 15. shake 16. bells 17. run 18. bone 19. suffered 20. foolish 21. energy 22. function 23. ashamed 24. mistake 25. promise

Invite the students to work in small groups to produce dialogues between different parts of the body, which they can present to the rest of the class. It should be apparent which parts of the body are speaking without having to mention them by name. The rest of the class can be asked to work out who's speaking to whom while listening to the presentations as a means of holding their attention. This activity is more appropriate for a higher level class, as is the final activity on the worksheet.

Now match the numbers with the letters to complete these proverbs about food and drink: 1-e / 2-j / 3-h / 4-a / 5-k / 6-d / 7-f / 8-i / 9-b / 10-c / 11-g

PARTS OF THE BODY

One day all the Limbs of the Body, the Arms and Legs, got together and complained to the Stomach: "We're sick and tired of doing all the work while you just eat everything we collect without paying for it and we've decided to go on strike." So the Feet refused to walk, the Hands stopped holding things, the Eyes avoided seeing, the Ears became deaf, the Nose stopped smelling and the Tongue refused to taste.

The Stomach was most upset because he couldn't get food from anywhere and didn't know what to do. Sometimes the best thing in such situations is to do nothing and that's exactly what the Stomach did. He just lay down patiently and waited.

He didn't have to wait very long because the Arms and the Legs quickly lost all their strength. The Hands began to shake and the Feet began to tremble. The Eyes began to cry, the Ears started to ring like bells, the Nose began to run and the Tongue was as dry as a bone.

When the Stomach saw they had suffered enough, he began to speak: "Now you can see how foolish you've been. I digested the food you gave me to produce the energy you need to function."

When the Limbs heard these words, they felt very ashamed of their actions. "You're right. We've been very stupid. We need you as much as you need us and we'll never make the mistake of complaining again. We promise. You can be sure we've learnt our lesson!"

PARTS OF THE BODY: WORKSHEET

Listen to the story and then decide what the moral is. If you don't like the suggestions given, find a moral of your own!

    a.   You can't live without food and water.
    b.   People need people.
    c.   Strikes serve no useful purpose.
    d.   When people work together, disagreements are inevitable.
    e.   The way to a man's heart is through his stomach.

Complete the story by putting the missing words below into the gaps:

avoided / ashamed / because / bells / bone / complained / deaf / energy / foolish / function / lay / limbs / lost / mistake / paying / promise / refused / run / shake / sick / situations / strike/ suffered / taste / upset /

One day all the 1. ….. of the Body, the Arms and Legs, got together and 2. ….. to the Stomach: "We're 3. ….. and tired of doing all the work while you just eat everything we collect without 4. ….., for it and we've decided to go on 5. …...." So the Feet 6. ….. to walk, the Hands stopped holding things, the Eyes 7. ….. seeing, the Ears became 8. ….., the Nose stopped smelling and the Tongue refused to 9. …...

The Stomach was most 10. ….. because he couldn't get food from anywhere and didn't know what to do. Sometimes the best thing in such 11. …... is to do nothing and that's exactly what the Stomach did. He just 12. ….. down patiently and waited.

He didn't have to wait very long13. …... the Arms and the Legs quickly 14. …..all their strength. The Hands began to 15. ….. and the Feet began to tremble. The Eyes began to cry, the Ears started to ring like 16. ….., the Nose began to 17. …. and the Tongue was as dry as a 18. …...

When the Stomach saw they had 19. …. enough, he began to speak: "Now you can see how 20. ….. you've been. I digested the food you gave me to produce the 21. …. you need to 22. …... ."

When the Limbs heard these words, they felt very 23. ….. of their actions. "You're right. We've been very stupid. We need you as much as you need us and we'll never make the 24 ….. of complaining again. We 25 ….. . You can be sure we've learnt our lesson!"

Now match the numbers with the letters to complete these proverbs about food and drink:

1	The proof of the pudding is	a. a free lunch.
2	The way to a man's heart is	b. better than none.
3	Too many cooks	c. get out of the kitchen
4	There's no such thing as	d. in one basket.
5	You can't make an omelette	e. in the eating.
6	Don't put all your eggs	f. into old bottles.
7	Don't put new wine	g. over spilt milk.
8	Don't bite the hand	h. spoil the broth.
9	Half a loaf is	i. that feeds you.
10	If you can't stand the heat	j. through his stomach.
11	It's not use crying	k. without breaking eggs.

THE MAN WHO ALWAYS SAID SHOULD

Level: Upper Intermediate / Advanced
Target Audience: Adults
Language / Skills Focus: Listening & Speaking. The modal verbs SHOULD & WOULD
Materials: Photocopies of the worksheets to hand out after the storytelling

IN CLASS

1. *Pre-listening:* You might like to discuss the following questions with the group as a lead-in to the tale.

   Can you accept people the way they are or are you always trying to change them?
   Is it possible to change the way people think by pressurizing them or do you believe we can only learn from our own mistakes?

2. *Post-listening:* Hand out copies of Worksheet 1. The matching activity deals with the new vocabulary presented in the story and the learners can work on it in pairs. The pairs can then be invited to form groups of four to compare their answers and thus reduce the likelihood of errors.

   Match the numbers on the left with the letters on the right to find explanations for the new vocabulary: 1-h / 2-o / 3-a / 4-n / 5-i / 6-j / 7-e / 8-d / 9-df / 10-b / 11-l / 12-p / 13-k / 14-g / 15-c

3. Ask the learners to make a list of all the things they think they should do. Allow a ten-minute time limit. Then ask them to reformulate the items in their lists by using the following wording: *If I really wanted to, I could .....*
   They will probably find some things now seem much more possible and there are other things which they now want to abandon. *Could* gives you choice!

4. Hand out copies of Worksheet 2, which is on the uses of SHOULD and WOULD. Instead of presenting the rules on a plate, it has been designed to give the class the opportunity to work out the rules for themselves.

Uses of SHOULD 1 / 2 / 8 / 9 / 11 / 12
Uses of WOULD 3 / 4 / 5 / 6 / 7 / 10

Fill in the gaps in the following passage with *should* or *would*, then compare your answers with the person sitting next to you: 1. should / 2. should / 3. would / 4. would / 5. would / 6. should / 7. should / 8. would / 9. would / 10. should / 11. should / 12. would / 13. would / 14. would / 15. should / 16. should / 17. would / 18. should / 19. would / 20. would

COMMENTS

Sometimes we can be our own worst enemies and place burdens on ourselves as a result of the language we use. *The Man Who Always Said Should* can be used to illustrate how this can happen. But by making use of techniques such as reformulation, we can change both our attitudes and our behaviour.

THE MAN WHO ALWAYS SAID SHOULD

He was always telling people what they should or shouldn't do and he knew best about everything. He didn't realize that *should* is probably the most damaging word in the English vocabulary. It implies you were wrong, you are wrong, or you're going to be wrong. What people really need is more choice in their lives, the choice offered by removing and replacing all *shoulds*.

At least you could say, he practised what he preached because he behaved the same way towards himself as he behaved towards everyone else. All the time the voice inside his own head was making statements about what he *should* and *shouldn't* do, how he *should* live his life and I suppose that's why he then imposed the same on others. Poor man. I wonder if he ever got any peace. Probably only when he was sleeping. And perhaps not even then. Who knows what he went through in his dreams? Probably constant torment. Not surprising then that he lost all his hair and ended up having a heart attack. But he didn't even learn from that. For once he'd recovered from the triple by-pass operation his condition necessitated, he started acting just as he had done before. In fact, if anything, he became even more unbearable. To put up with him you had to be a saint. And that's exactly what his dear wife was.

However, gradually through his constant criticism, he destroyed even her. He hammered away at her daily until she no longer had any mind of her own. Her actions became dictated by what she thought he believed she *should* or *shouldn't* do. That's when he lost interest in her and left her for another woman – someone else to mould into his likeness. Three days later she killed herself.

After that he became a changed man. He got himself committed to an asylum, which suited him just fine. He was drugged up to the eyeballs daily, his nagging inner voice was silenced forever, and he no longer had to make any choices at all. They were all made for him there.

I suppose he's found peace of mind of a kind. He spends his days sitting glued to the TV watching soap operas. The only choice to be made is which channel to watch. And he doesn't even have to make that decision as the nurse on duty does that for him. No more *shoulds* or *shouldn'ts* to worry about and that's the way he likes it - much safer by far.

THE MAN WHO ALWAYS SAID SHOULD: WORKSHEET 1

Match the numbers on the left with the letters on the right to find explanations for the new vocabulary:

1.	committed to an asylum	a. completely under the influence of medication
2.	constant torment	b. did what he told others to do
3.	drugged up to the eyeballs	c. experienced
4.	glued to	d. form into a copy of himself
5.	hammered away at	e. forced
6.	implies	f. giving advice in an annoying way
7.	imposed	g. intolerable
8.	mould to his likeness	h. obliged to undergo residential psychiatric treatment
9.	nagging	i. put pressure on
10.	practised what he preached	j. suggests
11.	soap operas	k. surgery to help the heart function more effectively
12.	suited him just fine	l. TV programmes broadcast several times a week about ordinary people
13.	triple by-pass operation	n. unable to separate oneself from
14.	unbearable	o. unhappiness all the time
15.	went through	p. was ideal for him

Make a list of all the things you think you should do. Give yourself a ten-minute time limit. The reformulate the items in your lists by using the following wording:

If I really wanted to, I could .....

You will probably find some things now seem much more possible and there are others which you now want to abandon. *Could* gives you choice!

Now discuss your findings, working in pairs or small groups.

THE MAN WHO ALWAYS SAID SHOULD: WORKSHEET 2

Working in pairs or small groups, decide which of the following points refer to uses of SHOULD and which of the following points refer to WOULD. Then place the points in the correct columns of the Table:

1. after certain adjectives (essential / surprised etc.)
2. after certain verbs (suggest / insist etc.)
3. to express criticism (I wish you ... keep picking your nose!)
4. for refusals (They ... not let their daughter have her navel pierced)
5. for things that happened habitually in the past and perhaps still do
6. to express attitudes you want others to adopt (The applicant ... have the interviewer believe that he's the most suitable person for the job even though he's never done this kind of work before)
7. to express surprise (You ... think they'd know better than to do that)
8. to give advice (If you want to lose weight, you ... go on a diet)
9. to make assumptions (Everyone says she's got a bright future so she ... get promotion in no time at all)
10. to make assumptions (It ... seem / appear that ...)
11. to point out inequalities (Why ... some people be rich while others have no money at all?)
12. to show surprise (I was walking through Hyde Park the other day when who ... I bump into but the Prime Minister)

Uses of SHOULD	Uses of WOULD

Fill in the gaps in the following passage with *should* or *would*, then compare your answers with the person sitting next to you:

Why 1. _____ some people find it easy to master a foreign language while others find it a struggle? And why 2. _____ some students succeed while other fail? It 3. _____ seem that there is no simple answer. However, if we were prepared to follow certain guidelines, we 4. _____ certainly be more likely to achieve good results. Advertisements for language courses 5. _____ have us believe that by some miraculous process we 6. _____ be able to attain fluency within a matter of weeks. Such claims 7. _____ be taken with a pinch of salt. There is no way you can learn a language overnight. It 8. _____ appear that the process is rather like climbing a mountain. There are times when you reach a plateau and it 9. _____ seem that you are getting nowhere. However, it is essential that you 10. _____ not get disheartened for soon you will start to climb again. The time you spend on the plateau 11. _____ be seen as a period of consolidation without which you 12. _____ be unable to move forward. You 13. _____ think that the more advanced you were, the faster your rate of progress 14. _____ be. However, progress is more noticeable at the lower levels as you move from being a zero beginner to being able to communicate in the language. It is only natural that you 15. _____ get frustrated at times and that you 16. _____ feel like giving up. After having put so much time and energy into the task, this 17. _____ be a great shame. It is recommended that you 18. _____ be prepared to experiment and to make mistakes as you can learn from your errors. If I were your teacher, I 19. _____ use the Direct Method and hardly ever let you talk in your own language. When I was at school I used to study French. Our teacher 20. _____ make us pay a fine whenever we spoke in English, which soon got us out of the habit!

THE GYPSY BOATMAN

Level: Pre-Intermediate / Intermediate
Target Audience: Adults
Language / Skills Focus: Listening & Speaking
Materials: Photocopies of the worksheet to hand out after the storytelling

IN CLASS

Pre-listening: How important is grammar? This question can be discussed in small groups as a pre-listening activity. Each group can then elect a spokesperson to present their views to the rest of the class.

While-listening: Read the story but omit the final line. Ask the listeners to predict what it is likely to be. They can then compare their suggestions with the original: ….. if you don't learn how to swim now, it's going to be the end of your life!"

Post-listening: Hand out the worksheet. Place the parts of the story in the correct order, and then complete the last part: 1-e / 2-i / 3-a / 4-g / 5-h / 6-b / 7-f / 8-c / 9-d

Now match the numbers with the letters to complete these proverbs about learning: 1-c / 2-a / 3-h / 4-d / 5-g / 6-e / 7-j / 8-b / 9-i / 10-f / 11-f

The Welsh tale that follows, like *The Gypsy Boatman*, can also be used to bring us back down to earth when we get too full of ourselves:

THE IMPORTANCE OF MIRACLES

There were once two brothers, Tomas and Wynford Davies, who lived in a village in the north of Wales. One day the elder of the two, Tomas, decided to dedicate his life to God, and departed for the bleak mountains of Snowdonia. He travelled deep into the wilderness and never looked back.

It was twenty-five, maybe thirty years later that Tomas Davies returned to his home. He was as thin as a skeleton, and his skin stretched taut over his sharp features. Yet he smiled when he recognised his brother and called out in a voice rusty from disuse, "Wynford, I have returned."

Wynford squinted at the emaciated vision before him. "My brother, is that really you? Where have you been all these years? You're a sight to make a man weep. But you must have learned something in all that time, or else you would have returned sooner."

"Three decades of living alone, fasting, and praying have given me the power to walk on water," Tomas smiled serenely.

"My poor brother," said Wynford, his heart filled with sorrow. "Have you really spent so many years on such foolishness? Why, when I want to cross the river, I only have to hail the ferryman, and I'm there in a matter of minutes."

You could follow up the Welsh story above by inviting the learners to consider the following question: Think of something you've spent a long time studying that turned out to be of little value. Tell the person sitting next to you about it.

Some people are so full of self-importance that they set themselves above the rest of us and we are equally to blame because we are prepared to bow down to them and to worship them as if they were Gods. The following tale can help to remedy the problem by enabling us to get things in perspective:

THE GYPSY BOATMAN

Once upon a time a grammarian went down to the seaside and decided to take a boat trip. So he rented a boat from a Gypsy. While the gypsy was rowing the boat, the grammarian asked him if he knew anything about literature or grammar.

The boatman answered that he'd never had time to learn how to read - he'd been too busy working and trying to feed his family to bother about such things. "I know my work, all there is to know about boats, and that's all I have to know."

The grammarian replied, "What a shame – you've wasted half your life with boats and know nothing about the more refined things in life."

Just then, all of a sudden, the weather changed, the sea got rough and things began to get scary. So the boatman asked the grammarian, "Hey, do you know how to swim?"

"No."

"Oh, what a shame – you've spent half your life studying literature and grammar and you never learnt how to swim?" Well, if

THE GYPSY BOATMAN: WORKSHEET

Place the parts of the story in the correct order, and then complete the last part:

a. "I know my work, all there is to know about boats, and that's all I have to know."

b. Just then, all of a sudden, the weather changed, the sea got rough and things began to get scary.

c. "No."

d. "Oh, what a shame – you've spent half your life studying literature and grammar and you never learnt how to swim?"

e. Once upon a time a grammarian went down to the seaside and decided to take a boat trip. So he rented a boat from a Gypsy.

f. So the boatman asked the grammarian, "Hey, do you know how to swim?"

g. The boatman answered that he'd never had time to learn how to read - he'd been too busy working and trying to feed his family to bother about such things.

h. The grammarian replied, "What a shame – you've wasted half your life with boats and know nothing about the more refined things in life."

i. While the gypsy was rowing the boat, the grammarian asked him if he knew anything about literature or grammar.

Well, if _____

_____

Now match the numbers with the letters to complete these proverbs about learning:

1 You can't teach
2 A little learning is
3 Don't try to teach your
4 Stupid is
5 A word is
6 Two heads are
7 The pen is
8 Great minds think
9 Practice
10 Those who do not learn from history are
11 Better to remain silent and be thought a fool than

a a dangerous thing.
b alike.
c an old dog new tricks.
d as stupid does.
e better then one.
f doomed to repeat it.
g enough to the wise
h Grandma to suck eggs.
i makes perfect.
j mightier than sword.
k to speak and remove all doubt.

WHY DOGS CHASE CATS

Level: Pre-Intermediate
Target Audience: Adults
Language / Skills Focus: Listening, Speaking, Creative Writing, and Use of the Tenses
Materials: Photocopies of the worksheets to hand out after the storytelling

IN CLASS

Pre-listening: Before reading the story to the class, ask the learners (working in small groups) to make a list everything cats and dogs have in common, and then to make a list of their differences. The lists produced by the different groups can then be compared and commented on.

While-listening: Ask the learners to find out why the dog got angry with the cat.

Post-listening: Hand out the worksheets and work through the activities. The answers to the exercises are presented below.

Reconstruct the story by putting the following sentences in the correct order:

1-g / 2-j / 3-f / 4-a / 5-h / 6-c / 7-I / 8-e / 9-k / 10-d / 11-b

Here are two animal jokes. Change the verbs in brackets into the correct tenses:

1 went 2 talks 3 looked 4 repeats 5 hears 6 decided 7 took 8 returned 9 have had 10 has not said
1 found 2 had escaped 3 rang 4 am just phoning 5 have just found 6 were 7 called 8 took 9 liked 10 do you recommend

Answer the clues across to complete the grid:

1 ridden / 2 breaks / 3 afraid / 4 parrot / 5 Before / 6 winter / 7 taller / 8 memory / 9 carrot / 10 travel / 11 rabbit

THE STORY

Once long ago, Dog was married to Cat. They were happy together, but every night when Dog came home from work, Cat said she was too sick to make him dinner. Dog was patient with this talk for a while, but he soon got fed up with making dinner for them both after a hard day's work. After all, Cat just stayed home all day long.

One day, Dog told Cat he was going to work, but instead he hid in the cupboard and watched Cat to see if she really was sick. As soon as Cat thought Dog had left, she started playing games with Kitten. They laughed and ran about. Cat wasn't the least bit sick.

Dog jumped out of the cupboard. When Cat saw him, she stuck a marble in her cheek and told Dog she had a toothache. Dog got so angry that he started chasing her around and around the house. And Dogs have been chasing Cats ever since.

WHY DOGS CHASE CATS: WORKSHEET (i)

Reconstruct the story by putting the following sentences in the correct order:

a.   After all, Cat just stayed home all day long.

b.   And Dogs have been chasing Cats ever since

c.   As soon as Cat thought Dog had left, she started playing games with Kitten.

d.   Dog got so angry that he started chasing her around and around the house.

e.   Dog jumped out of the cupboard.

f.   Dog was patient with this talk for a while, but he soon got fed up with making dinner for them both after a hard day's work.

g.   Once long ago, Dog was married to Cat.

h.   One day, Dog told Cat he was going to work, but instead he hid in the cupboard and watched Cat to see if she really was sick.

i.   They laughed and ran about. Cat wasn't the least bit sick.

j.   They were happy together, but every night when Dog came home from work, Cat said she was too sick to make him dinner.

k.   When Cat saw him, she stuck a marble in her cheek and told Dog she had a toothache.

1. __ 2. __ 3. __ 4. __ 5. __ 6. __ 7. __ 8. __ 9. __ 10. __ 11. __

Work in pairs. Ask each other the questions below, and then report back with the information you find out about your partner to the rest of the class:

a.   They say the English love animals more than children. Is this true or false in your opinion?

b.   What do you prefer – cats or dogs?

c.   If you were born again as an animal, which animal would you like to be, and why?

d.   What pets do you have, or did you have when you were a child?

e.   They latest research indicates that people who keep cats as pets have fewer heart attacks. Why do you think this is the case?

f.   How do you feel about blood sports like fox-hunting and bull-fighting?

g.   If you don't like the idea of killing animals, why don't you become a vegetarian?

h.   How do you feel about animals being kept in zoos or used in circuses – a good or a bad idea?

Working in small groups, now write collective stories about why cats chase mice. Then tell your stories to the rest of the class:

WHY DOGS CHASE CATS: WORKSHEET (ii)

Here are two animal jokes. Change the verbs in brackets into the correct tenses:

A man 1 _____ (go) to a pet shop to buy a parrot. He said "I hope it's a good one and it 2 _____ (talk)" The assistant 3 _____ (look) surprised. "Good? I guarantee that this bird 4 _____ (repeat) every word it 5 (hear)" So the customer 6 _____ (decide) to buy it and 7 _____ (take) the bird home. Three days later he 8 _____ (return) to the shop. He said "This bird's no god. I 9 _____ (have) him three days and he 10 _____ (not say) a word yet." The salesman said, "No, he's deaf."

A man 1 _____ (find) a chimpanzee sitting in his garden that 2 _____ (escape) from a pet shop. So he 3 _____ (ring) up the police and said "I 4 _____ just _____ (phone) to say I 5 _____ (just find) a chimpanzee." The policeman said, "If I 6 _____ (be) you sir, I'd take him to the zoo at once." The next day he 7 _____ (call) the police again. He said, I 8 _____ (take) the chimpanzee to the zoo and he 9 _____ (like) it very much. Where 10 _____ (you recommend) I should take him today?"

What animal jokes or funny stories about animals do you know? Get together in circles of four or eight and tell them to each other.

A LETTERGRAM Answer the clues across to complete the grid:

1	R					
2		R				
3			R			
4				R		
5					R	
6						R
7						R
8					R	
9				R		
10			R			
11		R				
12	R					

1 Have you ever _____ a camel? – Yes, I have. On holiday in Tunisia once.

2 Seeing animals badly treated _____ my heart.

3 Actually, I'm not _____ of snakes but I'm absolutely terrified of spiders.

4 a talking bird from tropical countries with bright-coloured feathers

5 _____ you try to stroke the dog, you'd better check to make sure it doesn't bite.

6 Certain animals hibernate in _____ and only wake up again when the weather gets warmer.

7 No other animal is _____than a giraffe and nothing is slower than a snail.

8 If you've got a _____ like an elephant, then you're very lucky because it means that you never forget anything.

9 One way of getting a donkey to do what you want is by offering it a _____ to eat.

10 I've got nothing against clowns or acrobats, but making animals perform in a _____ is cruel and I don't think it should be allowed.

11 If you want to see a Koala bear in its natural habitat, then you'll have to _____ to Australia.

12 Bugs Bunny is a famous one – they have big ears and like eating lettuce.

THE LAST LAUGH

Level: Upper Intermediate
Target Audience: Adults
Language / Skills Focus: Listening & Speaking
Materials: Photocopies of the worksheets to hand out after the storytelling

IN CLASS

Pre-listening: Find out what the learners know, if anything, about the Sufis and Mullah Nasrudin. They may surprise you. If not, by way of an introduction, tell them what you know.

While-listening: Ask the learners to find out why Nasrudin, despite the fact that he's dying, asks his wives to dress up in their very best clothes.

Post-listening: Hand out the worksheets with the ordering activity and the questions for pairwork interviews.

Reconstruct the story by putting the following sentences in the correct order: 1-c / 2-a / 3-f / 4-g / 5-e / 6-b / 7 d / 8-i / 9 h

COMMENTS

Few educated people in the West have not at least heard of the unbelievable, humorous exploits of Mullah Nasrudin, told in countless Muslim Sufi tales and *The Last Laugh* provides a good example.

It appears that Nasrudin was invented by Sufi teachers to conveniently make any number of points about life, death, and the great Beyond. In the tales, Nasrudin describes himself as being "upside down in this world." All authentic spirituality is a great reversal of ordinary values, attitudes, and actions. What the ordinary person deems to be of inestimable value (job, home, and family), the spiritual practitioner considers to be purely secondary. His or her heart is set on transcending all this, and on discovering what is truly and permanently real – call it God, Spirit, or Self. Nasrudin is a symbol for the Sufi path of inner change (metanoia) and reversal (Feurstein, G., *Holy Madness: the shock tactics and radical teachings of crazy-wise adepts, holy fools, and rascal gurus*, Paragon House, 1991, pp.14-15).

THE STORY

Nasrudin Hodja had grown old and was on his last legs. His two wives were heartbroken. They knew that his end was near so they decided, to suit the occasion, they should dress in mourning robes and veils to show their respect.

"What's this?" he said, seeing their sorrowful appearance. "Remove your veils, wash your faces and comb your hair. Make yourselves beautiful and put on your prettiest dresses."

"How could we do that?" asked the older of his wives, "with our dear husband on his deathbed?"

With a wry smile he replied, speaking more to himself than to them, "Perhaps when the Angel of Death makes his entry he'll see the two of you, all dressed up like young brides, and he'll take one of you instead of me."

With these final words he laughed quietly to himself, happily closed his eyes, and died.

THE LAST LAUGH: WORKSHEET

Reconstruct the story by putting the following sentences in the correct order:

a. His two wives were heartbroken.

b. "How could we do that?" asked the older of his wives.

c. Nasrudin Hodja had grown old and was on his last legs.

d. "Our dear husband is on his deathbed!"

e. "Remove your veils, wash your faces and comb your hair. Make yourselves beautiful and put on your prettiest dresses."

f. They knew that his end was near so they decided, to suit the occasion, they should dress in mourning robes and veils to show their respect.

g. "What's this?" he said, seeing their sorrowful appearance.

h. With these final words he laughed quietly to himself, happily closed his eyes, and died.

i. With a wry smile he replied, speaking more to himself than to them, "Perhaps when the Angel of Death makes his entry he'll see the two of you, all dressed up like young brides, and he'll take one of you instead of me."

1 ___ 2 ___ 3 ___ 4 ___ 5 ___ 6 ___ 7 ___ 8 ___ 9 ___

Work in pairs. Ask each other the following questions, then report back to the rest of the group with your findings:

a. How would you want to spend your last days if you knew that you were dying?
b. And how would you like the people around you to behave towards to you?
c. How would you like to be remembered when you die?
d. Would you like to live forever? Why or why not?
e. How do you feel about euthanasia?
f. Some people try to cheat the ageing process by having cosmetic surgery to make them look younger. Would you ever consider such procedures? Why or why not?
g. If you could change the way you look, what would you choose to change, and why?

RAINY DAY, SUNNY DAY

Level: Upper Intermediate
Target Audience: Adults
Language / Skills Focus: Listening & Speaking
Materials: Photocopies of the worksheets to hand out after the storytelling

IN CLASS

Pre-listening: The Buddhist parable you're about to listen to / read is about someone who can't stop worrying. What do you waste your time worrying about?

While-listening: Pause after the words "On sunny days, don't think of your elder daughter not being able to sell umbrellas but of the younger daughter …" and ask the listeners to anticipate the ending to the sentence.

Post-listening: What do you think of the monk's advice? How could you apply it to your own life?

Hand out the worksheets with the ordering activity and vocabulary check exercise

Reconstruct the story by putting the following parts in the correct order: 1-j / 2-d / 3-k / 4-a / 5-c / 6-e / 7-h / 8-f / 9-g / 10-l / 11-i / 12-b

Find words in the story which mean the same as: a. vendor b. grieved for / c. console / d. curious / e. your perspective / f. prosper / g. saw the light

THE STORY

There was once an old lady who cried all the time. Her elder daughter was married to an umbrella merchant while the younger daughter was the wife of a noodle vendor. On sunny days, she would worry, "The weather's so nice and sunny that nobody's going to buy any umbrellas. What will happen if the shop has to be closed?" These worries made her sad. She just could not help but cry. When it rained, she would worry for the younger daughter. "My younger daughter's married to a noodle vendor. You can't dry noodles without the sun so now there will be no noodles to sell. What should we do?" As a result, the old lady worried herself silly everyday. Whether it was sunny or rainy, she always grieved for one of her daughters. Her neighbours could not console her and jokingly called her "the crying lady."

One day, she met a monk. He was very curious as to why she was always crying. She explained the problem to him. The monk smiled kindly and said, "Madam! You needn't worry. I'll show you a way to happiness, and you'll never need to grieve any more."

The crying lady was very excited. She immediately asked the monk to show her what to do. The master replied, "It's very simple. You just need to change your perspective. On sunny days, don't think of your elder daughter not being able to sell umbrellas but of the younger daughter being able to dry her noodles. With such good strong sunlight, she must be able to make plenty of noodles and her business must be very good. When it rains, think about the umbrella store of the elder daughter. With the rain, everyone must be buying umbrellas. She'll sell a lot of umbrellas and her store will prosper."

The old lady saw the light. She followed the monk's instruction. After a while, she did not cry anymore; instead, she was smiling everyday. From that day on she was known as "the smiling lady."

RAINY DAY, SUNNY DAY: WORKSHEET

Reconstruct the story by putting the following parts in the correct order:

a.   As a result, the old lady worried herself silly everyday. Whether it was sunny or rainy, she always grieved for one of her daughters.

b.   From that day on she was known as "the smiling lady."

c.   Her neighbours could not console her and jokingly called her "the crying lady."

d.   On sunny days, she would worry, "The weather's so nice and sunny that nobody's going to buy any umbrellas. What will happen if the shop has to be closed?" These worries made her sad. She just could not help but cry.

e.   One day, she met a monk. He was very curious as to why she was always crying. She explained the problem to him.

f.   The crying lady was very excited. She immediately asked the monk to show her what to do.

g.   The master replied, "It's very simple. You just need to change your perspective. On sunny days, don't think of your elder daughter not being able to sell umbrellas but of the younger daughter being able to dry her noodles. With such good strong sunlight, she must be able to make plenty of noodles and her business must be very good.

h.   The monk smiled kindly and said, "Madam! You needn't worry. I'll show you a way to happiness, and you'll never need to grieve any more."

i.   The old lady saw the light. She followed the monk's instruction. After a while, she did not cry anymore; instead, she was smiling everyday.

j.   There was once an old lady who cried all the time. Her elder daughter was married to an umbrella merchant while the younger daughter was the wife of a noodle vendor.

k.   When it rained, she would worry for the younger daughter. "My younger daughter's married to a noodle vendor. You can't dry noodles without the sun so now there will be no noodles to sell. What should we do?"

l.   When it rains, think about the umbrella store of the elder daughter. With the rain, everyone must be buying umbrellas. She'll sell a lot of umbrellas and her store will prosper."

1 ___   2 ___   3 ___   4 ___   5 ___   6 ___   7 ___   8 ___   9 ___   10 ___   11 ___   12 ___

Find words in the story which mean the same as:

a.   someone who sells things

b.   was upset and concerned about

c.   comfort

d.   wanting to know why

e.   the way you look at things

f.   be successful

g.   learnt her lesson

THE MAN WHO BECAME RICH THROUGH A DREAM

Level: Upper Intermediate
Target Audience: Adults
Language / Skills Focus: Listening & Speaking
Materials: Photocopies of the worksheets to hand out after the storytelling

IN CLASS

Pre-listening: Ask the class if anyone has ever had a dream about something that then turned out to be true, and what we call dreams of this kind (premonitions).

While-listening: Ask the learners to find out what the wealthy businessman's dream was.

Post-listening: Hand out the worksheets with the ordering activity and the points for groupwork discussion.

Reconstruct the story by putting the following parts in the correct order: 1-g / 2-d / 3-i / 4-j / 5-f / 6-c / 7-a / 8-e / 9-k / 10-l / 11-h / 12-b

COMMENTS

The riches that we long for and travel far and wide in search of, can often be found where we least expect them to be - on our own doorstep - as the man in the following tale finds out. It has been adapted from a story in *The Book of the Thousand Nights and a Night,* translated by Richard F. Burton (London: The Burton Club, 1885). Since its first translation into a European language between 1704 and 1717, *The Thousand and One Nights,* also known as *The Arabian Nights,* has been recognized as a universal classic of fantasy narrative. It is, in fact, a much older work. Based on Indian, Persian, and Arab folklore, it dates back at least 1000 years as a unified collection, with many of its individual stories undoubtedly being even older. If this particular story seems familiar to you, it might be because it provided the basis for the modern classic - Paolo Coelho's *The Alchemist.*

THE STORY

Once there lived in Baghdad a wealthy businessman who lost all his means and was then forced to earn his living by hard labour. One night a man came to him in a dream, saying, "Your fortune is in Cairo; go there and seek it." So he set out for Cairo. He arrived there after dark and took shelter for the night in a mosque. As Allah would have it, a band of thieves entered the mosque in order to break into an adjoining house. The noise awakened the owners, who called for help. The Chief of Police and his men came to their aid. The robbers escaped, but when the police entered the mosque they found the man from Baghdad asleep there. They laid hold of him and beat him with palm rods until he was nearly dead, then threw him into jail.

Three days later the Chief of Police sent for him and asked, "Where do you come from?"

"From Baghdad," he answered.

"And what brought you to Cairo?"

"A man came to me in a dream and told me to come to Cairo to find my fortune," answered the man from Baghdad "But when I came here, the promised fortune proved to be the palm rods you so generously gave to me."

"You fool," said the Chief of Police, laughing until his wisdom teeth showed. "A man has come to me three times in a dream and has described a house in Baghdad where a great sum of money is supposedly buried beneath a fountain in the garden. He told me to go there and take it, but I stayed here. You, however, have foolishly journeyed from place to place, putting all your faith in a dream which was nothing more than a meaningless hallucination." He then gave him some money saying, "This will help you return to your own country."

The man took the money. He realized that the Chief of Police had just described his own house in Baghdad, so he returned home immediately, where he discovered a great treasure beneath the fountain in his garden. And this is how Allah brought the dream's prediction to fulfilment.

THE MAN WHO BECAME RICH THROUGH A DREAM: WORKSHEET

Reconstruct the story by putting the following parts in the correct order:

a. "A man came to me in a dream and told me to come to Cairo to find my fortune," answered the man from Baghdad.

b. And this is how Allah brought the dream's prediction to fulfilment.

c. "And what brought you to Cairo?"

d. As Allah would have it, a band of thieves entered the mosque in order to break into an adjoining house. The noise awakened the owners, who called for help. The Chief of Police and his men came to their aid.

e. "But when I came here, the promised fortune proved to be the palm rods you so generously gave to me."

f. "From Baghdad," he answered.

g. Once there lived in Baghdad a wealthy businessman who lost all his means and was then forced to earn his living by hard labour. One night a man came to him in a dream, saying, "Your fortune is in Cairo; go there and seek it." So he set out for Cairo. He arrived there after dark and took shelter for the night in a mosque.

h. The man took the money. He realized that the Chief of Police had just described his own house in Baghdad, so he returned home immediately, where he discovered a great treasure beneath the fountain in his garden.

i. The robbers escaped, but when the police entered the mosque they found the man from Baghdad asleep there. They laid hold of him and beat him with palm rods until he was nearly dead, then threw him into jail.

j. Three days later the Chief of Police sent for him and asked, "Where do you come from?"

k. "You fool," said the Chief of Police, laughing until his wisdom teeth showed. "A man has come to me three times in a dream and has described a house in Baghdad where a great sum of money is supposedly buried beneath a fountain in the garden. He told me to go there and take it, but I stayed here.

l. You, however, have foolishly journeyed from place to place, putting all your faith in a dream which was nothing more than a meaningless hallucination." He then gave him some money saying, "This will help you return to your own country."

1 ___ 2 ___ 3 ___ 4 ___ 5 ___ 6 ___ 7 ___ 8 ___ 9 ___ 10 ___ 11 ___ 12 ___

Working in small groups, discuss the following questions and then report back to the rest of the class:

a. If you had been the wealthy business man from Baghdad, what would you have done? Would you have followed your dream and gone to Cairo, or would you have ignored it and stayed at home instead?

b. Have you ever searched far and wide for a solution to a problem that was actually under your very nose all the time? Tell me about it.

c. If you found a chest of treasure, what would you do with it and why?

GUESTS

Level: Pre-Intermediate / Intermediate
Target Audience: Adults
Language / Skills Focus: Listening & Speaking
Materials: Photocopies of the worksheets to hand out after the storytelling

IN CLASS

Pre-listening: When was the last time you put someone up for the night? Was it inconvenient for you? And if so, why did you do it?

While-listening: Listen to the story to find out how the traveller gets a bed for the night.

Post-listening: Hand out the worksheets.

Reconstruct the story by putting the following parts in the correct order: 1-c / 2-j / 3-e / 4-f / 5-a / 6-g / 7-b / 8-h / 9-i / 10-d

COMMENTS

In some cultures friendship is valued more highly than anything else and it is believed that guests come from God. This story about the subject is a traditional tale from Lithuania.

THE STORY

A tired traveller was travelling past a rich gentleman's home as night fell, so he asked him if he could spend the night there.

"This isn't a hotel," said the rich gentleman angrily.

The tired traveller thought for a moment before replying, then said: "I'm sorry, but I'd like to know, who lived in this palace before you."

"My father did."

"And before your father?"

"My father's father."

"And who will live here after you?"

"My son I hope."

"So you see that people have often lived like guests here," the tired traveller pointed out. "And this palace really is like a hotel for people passing through."

At this the gentleman felt ashamed of the way he had behaved and ordered the palace's servant to allow the tired traveller to stay for as long as he liked.

GUESTS: WORKSHEET

Reconstruct the story by putting the following parts in the correct order:

a. "And before your father?"

b. "And who will live here after you?"

c. A tired traveller was travelling past a rich gentleman's home as night fell, so he asked him if he could spend the night there.

d. At this the gentleman felt ashamed of the way he had behaved and ordered the palace's servant to allow the tired traveller to stay for as long as he liked.

e. The tired traveller thought for a moment before replying, then said: "I'm sorry, but I'd like to know, who lived in this palace before you."

f. "My father did."

g. "My father's father."

h. "My son I hope."

i. "So you see that people have often lived like guests here," the tired traveller pointed out. "And this palace really is like a hotel for people passing through."

j. "This isn't a hotel," said the rich gentleman angrily.

1 ___ 2 ___ 3 ___ 4 ___ 5 ___ 6 ___ 7 ___ 8 ___ 9 ___ 10 ___

Work in pairs. Ask each other the questions below, and then report back with the information you find out about your partner to the rest of the class:

a. How would you react if a stranger knocked on your door and asked you to put him / her up for the night?

b. Would you ever behave like the tired traveller and ask a stranger to put you up for the night? If not, why?

c. How important are your friends to you – more important than your family or less important than your family?

d. How many friends do you have – enough, too few, or too many? And if you have too few or too many friends, why do you think that is?

e. How important is it to make guests feel at home in your culture?

f. Give a personal example of an occasion when a stranger was particularly hospitable (or unfriendly) towards you.

Working in small groups, make a list of all the different ways you can think of for making new friends. Then compare your list with those produced by the other groups. How many of these different ways have you tried, or are you prepared to try?

There are many different kinds of friend. You can have a pen friend, a close friend, a platonic friend, a childhood friend, a best friend, an old friend, a new friend, or an ex-friend. There are also false friends – people you think are friends but who turn out to be enemies. Choose one of these, someone you know, and then make some notes about them - about how you first met each other, his / her age, his / her appearance, and his / her character. Then, using your notes, tell the rest of the class about the person.

THE SACK

Level: Pre-Intermediate / Intermediate
Target Audience: Adults
Language / Skills Focus: Listening, Speaking & Informal Letter Writing
Materials: Photocopies of the worksheets to hand out after the storytelling

IN CLASS

Pre-listening: Ask those people in the class who feel that they have been unlucky in their lives to put their hands up. Then tell them that the story they are about to hear might make them change the way they feel.

While-listening: Ask the learners to find out why the man that the Mullah met was so upset, and what the Mullah did about the problem.

Post-listening: Hand out copies of the worksheets with the ordering activity, and the pair and group work.

Reconstruct the story by putting the following parts in the correct order:
1-c / 2-g / 3-d / 4-e / 5-a / 6-b / 7-h / 8-f

COMMENTS

The Sack is a Sufi Story from the Middle East which teaches us not to feel sorry for ourselves by showing what we have to be thankful for.

THE STORY

One day Mullah was walking along the road to town when he met a man who was clearly very upset. "What's wrong?" he asked.

The man held up an old bag and moaned, "All that I own in the whole wide world doesn't even fill this rotten old sack."

"Too bad," said Mullah, and with that, he snatched the bag from the man's hands and ran down the road with it.

Having lost everything, the man burst into tears and, more miserable than before, continued walking. Meanwhile, Mullah quickly ran around the corner and placed the man's sack in the middle of the road where he was sure to find it.

When the man saw his bag sitting in the road before him, he laughed with joy, and shouted, "My sack, thank God! I thought I'd lost you!"

Watching through the bushes, Mullah laughed and said. "Well, that's one way to make someone happy!"

THE SACK: WORKSHEET

Reconstruct the story by putting the following parts in the correct order:

a. Having lost everything, the man burst into tears and, more miserable than before, continued walking.

b. Meanwhile, Mullah quickly ran around the corner and placed the man's sack in the middle of the road where he was sure to find it.

c. One day Mullah was walking along the road to town when he met a man who was clearly very upset.

d. The man held up an old bag and moaned, "All that I own in the whole wide world doesn't even fill this rotten old sack."

e. "Too bad," said Mullah, and with that, he snatched the bag from the man's hands and ran down the road with it.

f. Watching through the bushes, Mullah laughed and said. "Well, that's one way to make someone happy!"

g. "What's wrong?" he asked.

h. When the man saw his bag sitting in the road before him, he laughed with joy, and shouted, "My sack, thank God! I thought I'd lost you!"

1 ___ 2 ___ 3 ___ 4 ___ 5 ___ 6 ___ 7 ___ 8 ___

Working in small groups, now choose a moral to go with the tale. And if you don't like any of the suggestions below, then choose one of your own:

:

a. Money doesn't grow on trees.
b. Things can always be worse.
c. Money talks.
d. Little things please little minds.
e. Money is the root of all evil.
f. Half a loaf is better than none.
g. Sometimes you need to be cruel to be kind.
h. Money makes the world go round.

Working on your own, make a list of everything you have to be thankful for. Then compare lists with the person sitting next to you. What was the most surprising item on your partner's list and what was the most predictable?

Write a letter to a friend who is feeling sorry for themselves. Do your best to cheer them up by pointing out all the good things they have in their lives.

THE FLOWER OF THE FERN

Level: Upper Intermediate
Target Audience: Adults
Language / Skills Focus: Listening, Speaking, & Story Writing (in groups)
Materials: Photocopies of the worksheets to hand out after the storytelling

IN CLASS

Pre-listening: For some people happiness is watching a beautiful sunset whereas for others it's having loads of money. What would your definition of happiness be? Tell the person sitting next to you about it.

Invite the learners to work in small groups, and give each group a copy of ten or twenty of the most important words in the story (the number being dependent on the level of the students), presented in the order in which they appear in the text (see the worksheet for this). Then invite each group to write a collective story using the words in the order given. Circulate to provide any assistance required. At the end, a spokesperson for each group can then present the story the group wrote to the rest of the class. Follow this by reading *The Flower of the Fern* to everyone so they can compare their versions with the original (Error correction and feedback on the collective stories, if required, can be left until the end of the lesson).

Post listening: Take a minute of clock time, equal to all the time you need, to consider all the reasons you have to be happy, to list all the good things in your life. Then turn to the person sitting next to you and share everything you have to be thankful for with him / her.

Tell the learners they are going to interview the writer of the story they have just read. Ask them to write three questions each after giving them an example of the kind of question you are looking for. They can then take it in turns to interview each other, with the interviewee taking on the role of the writer.

COMMENTS

Catholics all over Poland celebrate St John's Night, the subject of this story, on the 22nd of June, but the origins can be traced back to pagan times when the Slavic peoples considered this to be a time of rebirth. Many of the rituals that used to be enacted, such as jumping over bonfires, symbolized a cleansing of the soul.

THE FLOWER OF THE FERN: WORKSHEET

Working in small groups, write a collective story entitled *The Flower of the Fern* using the words presented below in the order given:

a boy called Janek
a small village in the middle of nowhere
poor
St John's Night
special clothes for the occasion
look for the flower of the fern
searched high and low for hours
"I can give you a fortune, but there is one condition."
"If you do, you will lose it forever."
a magnificent palace
the promise he had made
a life of luxury and ease
lonely and miserable
vanished into thin air
He finally understood

THE FLOWER OF THE FERN

Once upon a time a boy called Janek was born in a small village in the middle of nowhere. His family were so poor that they couldn't even afford to buy bread and they lived on a diet of oats and sour milk instead. In spite of their poverty, they were happy, worked hard and enjoyed life.

The years passed quickly and another spring was nearly over. Like every year, the whole community involved themselves in the preparations for St John's Night. The men and boys chopped wood for bonfires while the womenfolk made garlands of flowers, baked bread and prepared special clothes for the occasion.

Janek was probably looking forward to the celebrations more than anyone. This was the first year in his life that he was going to be allowed to look for the flower of the fern. It also meant he was no longer considered a child.

It was a warm summer evening and the whole community gathered on the banks of the river just outside the village. Bonfires everywhere illuminated the darkness, the air was filled with the fragrance of flowers and herbs, the womenfolk were dressed all in white, and the men wore their very best smocks. The atmosphere was special and everyone felt moved by the occasion.

The proceedings started with a prayer to mother earth, and then they sang and gave thanks to the four elements – earth, fire, air and water. Candles set in garlands of flowers were floated on the water, the musicians started playing and the young people were moved to dance. Meanwhile, the elders of the community sat around the fires and told stories to each other.

Janek, meanwhile, was waiting impatiently for midnight. When it finally came, he was the first of the young men to gather at the edge of the forest for the quest in search of the flower. Although nobody had ever found the legendary flower of the fern, there was absolutely no one at all who doubted its existence.

Each of the young men wanted to be the first and only person to find the flower so, on the stroke of midnight, they all set off in different directions. Janek, however, was the quickest and soon left the others far behind him. He tripped over many times, got stung by nettles and scratched by thorns, and even lost his straw hat in the process, but he kept on going regardless. Although he searched high and low for hours, there was no sign of the mystical flower at all. Totally exhausted and dispirited, he eventually gave up and started to make his way back to the village. Just then, all of a sudden, he noticed a light in the nearby bushes. He went over to the bush and, with trembling hands, parted the leaves to see what was shining so brightly. And there it was - the flower of the fern, in all its glory. Janek stared at it motionlessly. Then when he bent down to pick it up, he heard a voice.

"Wait! I am the flower of the fern and I can give you a fortune, but there is one condition."

"I'll do whatever you ask," whispered Janek, in awe of such power.

"I can give you everything, more than you have ever dreamt of, but on no account must you share your good fortune with anyone. If you do, you will lose it forever."

"That's easy," replied Janek confidently. "No problem at all."

As soon as he said that, the flower disappeared and, with it, the forest. Janek found himself in a magnificent palace, seated at a table, being served all kinds of delicacies, food he had never even seen before. He had a golden carriage with twelve white horses, servants, fancy clothes and so much food and drink that he didn't know what to do with it all. But because of the promise he had made, he knew he couldn't share it with anyone. After a while, he no longer cared about others anyway, so the promise he had made no longer troubled him.

Years passed and Janek lived a life of luxury and ease, travelling wherever he wanted to go, whenever he felt like it. Once, on his way back to the Palace, his horses became lost and he found himself in the middle of the countryside. He looked around him and strange thoughts came into his head that somehow he knew this place. A dilapidated hut in the distance caught his eye. He asked an old woman, who was passing by, all about the place.

"A poor but happy family used to live in that hut," she answered. "But many years ago, the son suddenly disappeared without any warning and broke his poor parents' hearts. They died soon afterwards."

And then it all came back to Janek – his family, the village, his childhood – and he broke down and cried. He finally understood how lonely and miserable he was despite all his riches. He took a handful of cold coins out of his pouch and placed them in the old woman's gnarled hands. At that moment, his carriage and horses vanished into thin air and he found sitting in the road dressed in rags. He finally understood, better late than never, that real happiness means giving and sharing, and has nothing to do with what you may possess or not.

THE CUCKOO (A CHECHEN FOLKTALE)

Level: Pre- Intermediate
Target Audience: Adults
Language / Skills Focus: Listening, Speaking & Writing
Materials: Photocopies of the worksheets to hand out after the storytelling

IN CLASS

Pre-listening: Is it our duty to look after our parents when they grow old or should they go into an Old People's Home? What normally happens in your country? Invite the learners to discuss these questions in small groups, and then to report back to the class with their findings. You can then tell them that the story they are going to hear offers a possible answer to the questions.

While-listening: Listen to the story to find out where cuckoos lay their eggs.

Post-listening: Hand out the worksheets.

Reconstruct the story by putting the following sentences in the correct order: 1-a / 2-f / 3-g / 4-d / 5-c / 6-b / 7-h / 8-e

Now fill the gaps in the following sentences with the correct form of either TO LAY or TO LIE: a. lay / b. lie / c. lying / d. lay / e. lies / f. lay / g. lay / h. lies / i. lay / j. laid

THE STORY

A long time ago there once lived a cuckoo with three small chicks. One day the Mother Cuckoo fell ill.

It's been said, that during her illness no one prepared any food for her, or brought her water. The cuckoo's children in fact did not look after their mother.

One time Mother Cuckoo said to her eldest child, 'Go and fetch me some water, I'm very thirsty.'

'But it's very cold outside and it's difficult for me to carry the water,' the eldest said refusing to do as her mother had asked.

And the other two didn't bring their mother a drop of water either.

So with all her remaining strength Mother Cuckoo flew away from the nest.

The children were alarmed. 'Come back! We will bring you water, feed you till you're full, we will help you with everything,' they cried.

However since then cuckoos don't know their parents and parents don't know their children. Cuckoos even lay their eggs in strangers' nests.

THE CUCKOO: THE WORKSHEET

Place the parts of the story in the correct order:

a. A long time ago there once lived a cuckoo with three small chicks. One day the Mother Cuckoo fell ill.

b. So with all her remaining strength Mother Cuckoo flew away from the nest.

c. And the other two didn't bring their mother a drop of water either.

d. 'But it's very cold outside and it's difficult for me to carry the water,' the eldest said refusing to do as her mother had asked.

e. However since then cuckoos don't know their parents and parents don't know their children. Cuckoos even lay their eggs in strangers' nests.

f. It's been said, that during her illness no one prepared any food for her, or brought her water. The cuckoo's children in fact did not look after their mother.

g. One time Mother Cuckoo said to her eldest child, 'Go and fetch me some water, I'm very thirsty.'

h. The children were alarmed. 'Come back! We will bring you water, feed you till you're full, we will help you with everything,' they cried.

1 _____ 2 _____ 3 _____ 4 _____ 5 _____ 6 _____ 7 _____ 8 _____

Now find a suitable moral for the tale from the list below. (If you find none of the suggested morals entirely suitable, then find one of your own).

a. Fine feathers make fine birds.

b. Don't bite the hand that feeds you.

c. Birds of a feather flock together.

d. One good turn deserves another.

e. A bird in the hand is worth two in the bush.

f. Sometimes you need to be cruel to be kind.

g. One swallow doesn't make a summer.

h. You scratch my back and I'll scratch yours.

From the story we learn that cuckoos *lay their eggs in strangers' nests*. TO LAY is a transitive verb. In other words it always takes an object. In this case the object is *eggs*. The three parts of the verb are LAY – LAID – LAID. TO LIE, on the other hand, is an intransitive verb and never takes an object: *If you're feeling lazy, you can lie in bed all day*. The verb is irregular and the three parts are LIE-LAY-LAIN.

Now fill the gaps in the following sentences with the correct form of either TO LAY or TO LIE:

a. When are you going to _____ the table for dinner? Your guests will be here soon and you haven't even started preparing thing yet.

b. How can you _____ there all day doing nothing? If I were you, I'd feel guilt, just watching everyone else do all the work.

c. The keys have been _____ there on the desk all morning. I think someone must have lost them.

d. There's no need for him to stand there holding the tray all the time. He can _____ it down on the table.

e. Perhaps the patient will feel more comfortable if she _____ on your side rather than on her back.

f. What we do now will hopefully _____ the foundations for the future success of the company.

g. There's a space over there by the pool where you can _____ your towel, next to the coconut tree.

h. The final decision _____ with you. Nobody else can make it for you.

i. Apparently the dead body _____ there for weeks before anybody found it.

j. If you had _____ a carpet on the floor instead of covering it with tiles, it would have made the room a lot warmer.

The story offers an explanation as to why cuckoos do not seem to know their parents and parents do not know their children. Working in small groups, write collective stories to explain the reasons for one of the following:

a. Why Dalmatians Have Spots
b. Why Camels Have Humps
c. Why Giraffes Have Long Necks
d. Why Manx Cats Have No Tails

THE ORIGIN OF STRAWBERRIES

Level: Upper Intermediate
Target Audience: Adults
Language / Skills Focus: Listening, Speaking & Writing / Collective Nouns
Materials: Photocopies of the worksheets to hand out after the storytelling

IN CLASS

Pre-listening: When you have a quarrel with your partner who usually says sorry or makes the peace first – you, your partner, or you hardly ever quarrel? Now listen to the story to find out what happened when the first man and his mate were created, and they had an argument with each other:

While-listening: Make a note of how many different types of berry are named in the story.

Post-listening: Hand out the worksheets. The learners can work on the activities individually, and then pair up or get into groups to compare their answers.

Reconstruct the story by putting the following sentences in the correct order: 1-i / 2-h / 3-c / 4-g / 5-a / 6-d /7-f / 8-e / 9-b

Match the collective nouns on the left with what they refer to on the right: 1-f or 1-d / 2-c / 3-i / 4-b / 5-l / 6-k / 7-d or 7-f/ 8-e / 9-j / 10-g / 11-h / 12-a

COMMENTS

The Cherokee (who call themselves the Tsalagi) originally occupied a large portion of the Alleghany mountains. Their territory covered the present-day states of Virginia, Tennessee, North Carolina, South Carolina, Georgia, and Alabama. In 1839, after a long series of conflicts with the US Government during which they were pushed westward towards the Mississippi, the Cherokees were forcibly evicted from their land and marched to Oklahoma in the dead of winter by the US Army. This is today known as the "Trail of Tears", one of the most shameful actions ever taken by the Unites States government, and possibly for this reason, the Cherokee tribe has become a focal point for a lot of white guilt.

The *Myths of the Cherokee*, excerpted from the 19th Annual Report of the Bureau of American Ethnology, is a nineteenth century collection of Cherokee myths, legends and folklore by the noted anthropologist James Mooney (1861-1921), who lived for several years with the Cherokee.

THE STORY

When the first man was created and a mate was given to him, they lived together very happily for a time, but then began to quarrel, until at last the woman left her husband and started off toward Nûñâgûñ'yï, the Sun land, in the east. The man followed alone and grieving, but the woman kept on steadily ahead and never looked behind, until Une''länûñ'hï, the great Apportioner (the Sun), took pity on him and asked him if he was still angry with his wife. He said he was not, and Une''länûñ'hï then asked him if he would like to have her back again, to which he eagerly answered yes.

So Une''länûñ'hï caused a patch of the finest ripe huckleberries to spring up along the path in front of the woman, but she passed by without paving any attention to them. Farther on he put a clump of blackberries, but these also she refused to notice. Other fruits, one, two, and three, and then some trees covered with beautiful red service berries, were placed beside the path to tempt her, but she still went on until suddenly she saw in front a patch of large ripe strawberries, the first ever known. She stooped to gather a few to eat, and as she picked them she chanced to turn her face to the west, and at once the memory of her husband came back to her and she found herself unable to go on. She sat down, but the longer she waited the stronger became her desire, for her husband, and at last she gathered a bunch of the finest berries and started back along the path to give them to him. He met her kindly and they went home together (from *Myths of the Cherokee* by James Mooney). From Nineteenth Annual Report of the Bureau of American Ethnology 1897-98, Part I. [1900] Scanned at www.sacred-texts.com, January-February 2001, and in the public domain).

THE ORIGIN OF STRAWBERRIES: WORKSHEET

Reconstruct the story by putting the following sentences in the correct order:

a. Farther on he put a clump of blackberries, but these also she refused to notice.

b. He met her kindly and they went home together

c. He said he was not, and Une'`länûñ'hï then asked him if he would like to have her back again, to which he eagerly answered yes.

d. Other fruits, one, two, and three, and then some trees covered with beautiful red service berries, were placed beside the path to tempt her, but she still went on until suddenly she saw in front a patch of large ripe strawberries, the first ever known.

e. She sat down, but the longer she waited the stronger became her desire, for her husband, and at last she gathered a bunch of the finest berries and started back along the path to give them to him.

f. She stooped to gather a few to eat, and as she picked them she chanced to turn her face to the west, and at once the memory of her husband came back to her and she found herself unable to go on.

g. So Une'`länûñ'hï caused a patch of the finest ripe huckleberries to spring up along the path in front of the woman, but she passed by without paving any attention to them.

h The man followed alone and grieving, but the woman kept on steadily ahead and never looked behind, until Une'`länûñ'hï, the great Apportioner (the Sun), took pity on him and asked him if he was still angry with his wife.

i. When the first man was created and a mate was given to him, they lived together very happily for a time, but then began to quarrel, until at last the woman left her husband and started off toward Nûñâgûñ'yï, the Sun land, in the east.

1 _____ 2 _____ 3 _____ 4 _____ 5 _____ 6 _____ 7 _____ 8 _____ 9 _____

We say *a group of people* but *a patch of huckleberries* or *strawberries,* and *a clump of blackberries.* Match the collective nouns on the left with what they refer to on the right:

1.	a bank of	a. coastline
2.	a bed of	b. earth
3.	a carpet of	c. flowers
4.	a clod of	d. fog
5.	a cloud of	e. fruit trees
6.	a dune of	f. grass
7.	a patch of	g. hills
8.	an orchard of	h. ice
9.	a puddle of	i. leaves
10.	a range of	j. rainwater
11.	a sheet of	k. sand
12.	a stretch of	l. smoke

1 ___ 2 ___ 3 ___ 4 ___ 5 ___ 6 ___ 7 ___ 8 ___ 9 ___ 10 ___ 11 ___ 12 ___

Sometimes arguments can lead to positive results if we learn something from them – either about ourselves or about the people we argue with. When has something like this happened to you? Tell the person next to you about it, and / or write an account of the argument and what happened as a result of it for homework.

Alternatively, you might like to rewrite the story, giving it a different ending in which the woman keeps on walking and perhaps meets someone else!

THE CHIEF AND THE WANDERER

Level: Pre-Intermediate / Intermediate
Target Audience: Adults
Language / Skills Focus: Listening, Speaking & 2nd Conditional
Materials: Photocopies of the worksheets to hand out after the storytelling

IN CLASS

Pre-listening: You could start with a brainstorming session to find out what the learners know about the place where the story comes from. The learners could be asked to prepare this in advance of the lesson, and they could do so by carrying out an internet search.

Post-listening: Hand out the worksheets. The learners can work on the activities individually, and then pair up or get into groups to compare their answers.

Reconstruct the story by putting the following sentences in the correct order: 1-a / 2-f / 3-h / 4-d / 5-g / 6-b /7-c / 8-e

COMMENTS

The Chief and the Wanderer is a traditional Dargi folktale. Known as the "land of the mountains," Dagestan lies immediately north of the Caucasus Mountains, and stretches for approximately 250 miles along the west shore of the Caspian Sea. It has been described as "the tip end of Europe. The Caucasus range is the boundary between the two continents, … and the wall of separation between the Christian and the Mohammedan worlds" (Curtis, 1911, p.228). Today, however, the situation is of course not so clear cut. With its mountainous terrain making travel and communication difficult, Dagestan is still largely tribal and, unlike in most other parts of Russia, the population (2,576,531 in 2002) is rapidly growing. There are 31 distinct ethnic groups, each with its own language, and Avar is the most widely spoken with about 700,000 speakers. To give some idea of the problems caused by the linguistic mix, despite the fact that Dargi and Avar are neighbours they are in fact mutually incomprehensible languages.

THE STORY

A tribal chief met a wanderer.

The chief said: "You've been to a lot of places, you've met a lot of people, tell me a good story."

"There's no better story on earth than about man's death," said the wanderer.

"That's not the kind of story I want to hear" said the chief in anger. "Tell me another one," said the ruler.

"The fact that a man who dies doesn't return for a second time is a good one too," said the wanderer. But this story didn't make the chief happy either.

"Leave my house, for you've told me nothing but bad stories - stories that nobody would want to hear," said the chief.

"Let me stay until I tell you another story," said the wanderer. "Listen boss, if the people didn't die, then all the chiefs born before you would still be here. And if they were present, where would you be then? For if all the dead rulers came back to life again, they would surely rise up and wouldn't let you carry on being in charge as you are - instead they would probably try to destroy you."

The chief became happy when he heard this and let the wanderer stay in his house for as long as he wanted to - now that he understood how lucky he was!

THE CHIEF AND THE WANDERER: WORKSHEET

Reconstruct the story by putting the following sentences in the correct order:

a. A tribal chief met a wanderer.

b. "Leave my house, for you've told me nothing but bad stories - stories that nobody would want to hear," said the chief.

c. "Let me stay until I tell you another story," said the wanderer. "Listen boss, if the people didn't die, then all the chiefs born before you would still be here. And if they were present, where would you be then? For if all the dead rulers came back to life again, they would surely rise up and wouldn't let you carry on being in charge as you are - instead they would probably try to destroy you."

d. "That's not the kind of story I want to hear" said the chief in anger. "Tell me another one," said the ruler.

e. The chief became happy when he heard this and let the wanderer stay in his house for as long as he wanted to - now that he understood how lucky he was!

f. The chief said: "You've been to a lot of places, you've met a lot of people, tell me a good story."

g. "The fact that a man who dies doesn't return for a second time is a good one too," said the wanderer. But this story didn't make the chief happy either.

h. "There's no better story on earth than about man's death," said the wanderer.

1 _____ 2 _____ 3 _____ 4 _____ 5 _____ 6 _____ 7 _____ 8 _____ 9 _____

Work in groups. Discuss the following questions, then choose a representative to report back to the rest of the class with your findings:

a. Who do you know who has lots of stories to tell?
b. Why do you think that is?
c. What's the secret to being able to tell a good story?
d. What story have you heard recently that perhaps led to you re-evaluating your life? Tell the person sitting next to you about it.

Continue the following line of speculation:

If people didn't die, the world would be overcrowded. If the world were overcrowded ...

Now do the same with the following:

If people didn't die, we wouldn't miss them. If we didn't miss them...

When you have finished, in groups of four, compare your endings with the endings of the others in your group.

THE CHILD OF GOD

Level: Upper Intermediate
Target Audience: Adults
Language / Skills Focus: Listening & Speaking
Materials: Photocopies of the story / worksheet to hand out after the storytelling

IN CLASS

Pre-listening: The story is set at the base of a Sacred Mountain. Are there any mountains considered to be sacred in your country, or do you know of any such places?

While-listening: Pause after "Well, to be completely honest with you, there is one child left. But ..." and ask the learners to predict what God said next. Then pause after "If they had, they would have seen ..." and ask the learners to predict what it was.

Post-listening: Hand out the photocopies. Ask the learners to work through the exercise under the story individually, and then to compare their answers in pairs or small groups.

Find words in the story which mean the same as: a. pre-ordained / b. gathered / c. long-anticipated ceremony / d. far and wide / e. side-tracked / f. pleaded / g. watch over us / h. be aware of how committed we are / i. to be completely honest with you / j. prematurely / k. staked her claim / l. to develop and thrive / m. followed his instructions to the letter / n. entrusted to their safekeeping

COMMENTS

If you were unable to have children, would you consider adopting instead? Why or why not? Would you tell your child he / she was adopted and, if so, when? Do you think single parents or gay couples should be allowed to adopt children? Why or why not? - These are just some of the questions that you might like to discuss with the class after telling the tale.

THE CHILD OF GOD: WORKSHEET

The pre-ordained date finally came round again and everyone gathered in a circle at the foot of Sacred Mountain, waiting for the sun to rise and the long-anticipated ceremony to commence.

The people came from far and wide and from all walks of life. But what all the couples shared was a common purpose – to be present for the Allocation Ceremony at which the newly born would be handed out.

Khatuna was late as usual. She'd got side-tracked along the way, stopping to help out an elderly compatriot who'd injured herself in a fall. So by the time Khatuna and her man reached the site, all the babies had already been allocated, all the couples had already dispersed, and God was already packing his bags and making preparations for his journey home.

Khatuna and Irakli were devastated. They'd been waiting all year for this day to come round and now they'd missed their one and only chance.

God was distressed too for he knew how much this day had meant to them and of all the trouble they had gone to in order to obtain the necessary paperwork to attend.

"I just wish there was something I could do to help you both," God sighed. "But I can't give you what I haven't got."

"Please God. There must be something you can do," Khatuna pleaded. "I know it's not for us to judge who's worthy to be a parent. But you who know us better than we know ourselves, you who watch over us as we go about our daily tasks, must surely be aware of how committed we are to parenthood and how seriously we would take our duties."

"Well, to be completely honest with you, there is one child left. But he was born prematurely so I put him to one side."

Without any hesitation, Khatuna boldly stepped forward and staked her claim. "Our love and dedication will provide the child with all he could possibly need to develop and thrive."

"Yes. I truly believe it will. Take the infant with my blessing. But there's one condition attached," God added. "Don't turn to look back on me after you leave. For, if you do so, then all will be lost."

It was not for Khatuna and Irakli to question their Lord and of course they followed his instructions to the letter.

But what if they had looked back? If they had, they would have seen God crying because he'd entrusted to their safekeeping his one and only son.

Find words in the story which mean the same as:

a arranged in advance / b assembled / c the event everyone had been waiting for / d lots of different places / e distracted / f begged him / g keep an eye on us / h know how dedicated we are / i to tell you the truth / j earlier than is the norm / k explained why she should be chosen rather than someone else / l grow up and do well / m did exactly what they were told to do / n considered them competent enough to look after

WHY UP THERE? (A traditional tale from Daghestan)

Level: Intermediate
Target Audience: Adults
Language / Skills Focus: Listening, Speaking & Phrasal Verbs (look up to / look down on)
Materials: Photocopies of the worksheets to hand out after the storytelling

IN CLASS

Pre-listening: You could start with a brainstorming session to find out what the learners know about the place where the story comes from. The learners could be asked to prepare this in advance of the lesson, and they could do so by carrying out an internet search.

Post-listening: Hand out the worksheets. The learners can work on the ordering activity individually, and then pair up or get into groups to compare their answers.

Reconstruct the story by putting the following sentences in the correct order: 1-f / 2-g / 3-d / 4-e / 5-b / 6-a /7-h / 8-c

COMMENTS

Known as the "land of the mountains," Dagestan lies immediately north of the Caucasus Mountains, and stretches for approximately 250 miles along the west shore of the Caspian Sea. It was described by Curtis (1911) as "the tip end of Europe. The Caucasus range is the boundary between the two continents, … and the wall of separation between the Christian and the Mohammedan worlds." Today, however, the situation is of course not so clear cut. With its mountainous terrain making travel and communication difficult, Dagestan is still largely tribal and, unlike in most other parts of Russia, the population (2,576,531 in 2002) is rapidly growing. There are 31 distinct ethnic groups, each with its own language, and Avar is the most widely spoken with about 700,000 speakers. To give some idea of the problems caused by the linguistic mix, despite the fact that Dargi and Avar are neighbours they are in fact mutually incomprehensible languages.

THE STORY

The very first meeting of Malla Nasradin and the chief is usually spoken about in the following way:

They say the chief invited Malla Nasradin into his castle. Malla Nasradin arrived and when he looked, he saw that the house was filled with people, all sitting on the floor in a circle.

Only the chief apparently sat on a very high chair, towering so high above everyone else that they had to strain their necks just to be able to see him.

The mullah gave his regards to the chief, saying 'May you be healthy, God!'

'I'm not God,' answered the chief, 'I'm ...'

But Malla Nasradin did not let him finish speaking: 'For you I'm prepared to give my life, Holy One!'

'What on earth are you talking about?' said the chief. What kind of Holy One am I?'

'I don't know,' answered Malla Nasradin, 'but if you're neither God, nor a Holy One, then why aren't you sitting down like the rest of the people, and why, instead, are you sitting up there in the sky?'

WHY UP THERE? WORKSHEET

Reconstruct the story by putting the following sentences in the correct order:

a) But Malla Nasradin did not let him finish speaking: 'For you I'm prepared to give my life, Holy One!'

b) 'I'm not God,' answered the chief, 'I'm ...'

c) 'I don't know,' answered Malla Nasradin, 'but if you're neither God, nor a Holy One, then why aren't you sitting down like the rest of the people, and why, instead, are you sitting up there in the sky?'

d) Only the chief apparently sat on a very high chair, towering so high above everyone else that they had to strain their necks just to be able to see him.

e) The mullah gave his regards to the chief, saying 'May you be healthy, God!'

f) The very first meeting of Malla Nasradin and the chief is usually spoken about in the following way:

g) They say the chief invited Malla Nasradin into his castle. Malla Nasradin arrived and when he looked, he saw that the house was filled with people, all sitting on the floor in a circle.

h) 'What on earth are you talking about?' said the chief. What kind of Holy One am I?'

1 _____ 2 _____ 3 _____ 4 _____ 5 _____ 6 _____ 7 _____ 8 _____

Work in pairs. Ask each other the following questions, and then report back to the rest of the class:

a. Have people been known to look up to you? If so, then why? In other words, what have they looked up to you for?
b. Who do you look up to, and why?
c. Who do you look down on, and why?
d. Are some of us better than others, are we all equal, or are some of us more equal than others?

IN THE GREENHOUSE

Level: Upper Intermediate to Advanced
Target Audience: Adults
Language / Skills Focus: Listening & Speaking
Materials: Photocopies of the story / worksheet to hand out after the storytelling

IN CLASS

Pre-listening: Some people talk to their plants or play music to them because they believe it helps them to grow better. Ask the class what they think of the idea as a lead-in to the tale. Alternatively, you could invite the learners to consider the following questions, in pairs or small groups, and then report back to the class with their findings: How do you tend to get on with the people you work with? Do you work together well as a team or does there tend to be a lot of in-fighting? What can be done to solve problems such as this?

While-listening: Pause after "He rushed outside, still in his pyjamas, to see what the problem was and he found … "and ask the learners to predict what.

Post-listening: Hand out the photocopies. Ask the learners to work through the exercise under the story individually, and then to compare their answers in pairs or small groups.

Find words in the story which mean the same as: a. succulent / b. tended / c. blessed with / d. a heated argument / e. almost coming to blows / f. get themselves into a state / g. gradually fade away / h. a chance to take effect / i. forthcoming / j. generally regarded as / k. a hush descended over the greenhouse / l. bowed their heads in shame

The questions presented below are multi-purpose in that they can be used for a post-listening activity with any story you choose to tell. And they are learner-centred, rather than teacher-centred, in that the students select the questions that interest them and then question each other. (This activity has been adapted from one suggested in an article by Mario Rinvolucri in the IATEFL Newsletter *Voices*, August 2008).

Choose three of the following questions to ask the person sitting next to you. Then report back what you found out to the rest of the class:

a.   What feelings did you have during the telling of the story?
b.   Have you ever been in a similar situation to any of the characters in the tale?
c.   Did any of the characters remind you of people you know?
d.   What do you think the "message" of the story is?
e.   Did it remind you of any other stories you know?

f. Which was the most moving or memorable bit of the story for you?

g. Which bit of the story sent you off to sleep?

COMMENTS

As a follow-up activity, you could find out what relaxation techniques the learners are familiar with, and then invite them up to the front to teach them to you and their classmates.

IN THE GREENHOUSE: WORKSHEET

Gilbert Greensleeves was very proud of his tomato collection and his succulent, perfectly formed specimens regularly won him prizes in horticultural competitions all over the land. He tended his plants as if they were his babies and, in a way, they were as Gilbert and his wife had never been blessed with any children of their own. So he was most upset when he woke up one fine summer morning to find a terrible commotion going on in the greenhouse.

He rushed outside, still in his pyjamas, to see what the problem was and he found all the tomatoes having a heated argument. In fact, the dispute had got so out of hand that the tomatoes were almost coming to blows. He tried to calm them all down and to make them see sense but without success and was at a total loss as to what to do.

Fortunately, he knew a bit about relaxation techniques, which he'd learnt to help him cope with his pre-competition nerves, and in desperation he decided to try them out on his beauties. After all, he didn't want them to get themselves into a state, especially just before the annual finals. It wasn't easy but he eventually managed to attract their attention and to persuade them all to follow his instructions.

"Good. Now I'd like you make yourselves comfortable and close your eyes," he began. "Feel the tension gradually fade away from the tops of your juicy heads to the tips of your little green toes." Here he paused for a moment to give his words a chance to take effect and to produce the desired results. "Now focus on your heads," he continued "and become aware of the fibre that extends from your crown chakra and what it's connected to."

After a couple of minutes, one of the more forthcoming tomatoes, generally regarded as the leader of the pack, broke the silence. "But we're all connected to each other and we all come from the same source," he observed.

"That's it exactly," Gilbert Greensleeves replied. "So now you've solved one of the mysteries of life. When you fight against each other, you're only fighting against yourselves. And perhaps now you can be more understanding and tolerant towards one another in future." A hush descended over the greenhouse as all the tomatoes bowed their heads in shame. It was clear that they had all learnt their lesson and Gilbert returned to the house with his head held high, his mission having been accomplished.

And from that moment onwards, Gilbert Greensleeves never had another problem. His tomatoes lived in perfect harmony and won him even more prizes than before!

***

Find words in the story which mean the same as:

a full of juice / b looked after / c lucky enough to have / d an enormous row / e on the point of hitting each other / f become agitated / g disappear slowly but surely / h time to work / i extrovert and outspoken / j by and large considered to be / k they all finally quietened down / l showed remorse for their actions

Choose three of the following questions to ask the person sitting next to you. Then report back what you found out to the rest of the class:

a.   What feelings did you have during the telling of the story?
b.   Have you ever been in a similar situation to any of the characters in the tale?
c.   Did any of the characters remind you of people you know?
d.   What do you think the "message" of the story is?
e.   Did it remind you of any other stories you know?
f.   Which was the most moving or memorable bit of the story for you?
g.   Which bit of the story sent you off to sleep?

THE TOWN OF STONE (a traditional tale from Armenia)

Level: Upper Intermediate
Target Audience: Adults
Language / Skills Focus: Listening & Speaking
Materials: Photocopies of the story to hand out after the storytelling

IN CLASS

Pre-listening: There are fairy stories about petrification, characters turning into stone, and there is also the example of Lot's wife in the Old Testament of the Bible. In the story you're about to hear it happens to a whole town of people. What do you suppose is the reason for this? Now listen to your teacher read the story to find out if you guessed correctly or not:

While-listening: Pause after the words "But, as he lifted it off her head..." and ask the learners to predict what follows.

Post-listening: Which famous public figure, current or historical, would you like to see turned into stone, and why? Give reasons for the choice or choices you make.

Which public figure, current or historical, would you like to see a statue of in the town or city you come from, and why? You might then like to draft a letter to the Editor of your local newspaper to start a public campaign for this statute to be built (This could be set as a possible homework assignment).

The desire to take revenge on the people who have made us suffer can be very strong at times. How do you feel about the belief in "an eye for an eye and a tooth or a tooth" being the perfect form of justice?

COMMENTS

Armenia, where this story originally came from, is the smallest of the former Soviet republics, and is bounded by Georgia in the north, Azerbaijan in the east, Iran in the south, and Turkey in the west. Frequently referred to as one of the cradles of civilization, it is also considered by many to have been the first country in the world to officially embrace Christianity as its religion (c. 300).

The Town of Stone

There was once an Armenian king, a ruler of a little town, who did not believe in God. "Who is God?" he would say to anyone who tried to change his mind.

No one was able to persuade the king, and because of his disbelief, the people of the town suffered. For ten years not one drop of rain fell, and vegetation of all kinds ceased to grow. The sheep could not find grass to graze and were dying. The people became hungry, and yet there was nothing they could do. They killed such animals as they had and ate them, but soon these, too, were all gone.

One day the people saw a strange thing happening among them. Many of them were slowly turning to stone, starting from their feet and moving upward. Soon all the people had become completely petrified. Then the king grew frightened that he, too, would turn to stone. "Guards," he ordered, "arrange everything so that the queen, myself and all my guards can climb that tall mountain and run away from this disease."

Very soon the king, the queen and all the king's guards, laden with food and tents, climbed the mountain in an attempt to get away from the disease. But do you think they could run away from God? No, they could not because God is everywhere.

Very soon the king began to turn to stone, starting from his feet. The queen was afflicted next and then the soldiers. In their foolishness they had imagined that they could hide from God, but not one of them was saved.

One day a traveller passing through the town saw that all the people had turned to stone. Surprised, he climbed the mountain near the town, and there he saw the king, the queen and all their guards standing as stones. He saw the beautiful crown which the queen had worn and decided to take it back home with him. But, as he lifted it off her head, it crumbled into dust. The man, seeing the danger that could come to him, left it there and ran as fast as he could down the mountain.

As far as we know, that town is still in existence, and the people in it are still petrified. And if a person should climb the mountain near the town, he would find the king, and the queen and all their guards, standing as quietly as stones (adapted from a tale told by Mrs. Mariam Serabian that was taken from Hoogasian-Villa, S., 1966, *100 Armenian Tales*, Detroit, Michigan: Wayne State University Press)

THE DREAMS OF A KING

Level: Upper Intermediate to Advanced

Target Audience: Adults

Language / Skills Focus: Listening, Speaking, and the preposition BY followed by ING to answer the question HOW

Materials: Photocopies of the story / worksheet to hand out after the storytelling

IN CLASS

Pre-listening: What do you suppose the dreams of a king would be about, and what can we do to help us remember our dreams? Possible answers might include hanging up a Dream catcher above the bed, or keeping a dream journal. You could ask these questions to the class as a whole or they could be discussed in pairs or small groups.

While-listening: Pause after "As an expert on the folklore of trees, surely his trusted and loyal servant would be able to interpret the meaning of the dream and so put an end to his suffering" and ask the learners to predict what the Head Gardener's interpretation of the King's dream was.

Post-listening: Hand out the photocopies. Ask the learners to work through the activities under the story individually, and then to compare their answers in pairs or small groups.

Find words in the story which mean the same as: a. plagued by a recurrent nightmare b. Despite his enormous wealth c. compensate for his discomfort d. went to great pains to ensure e. At his wits end f. Being a renowned gourmet g. regardless of whether it met with royal approval or not h. stuffing themselves silly i. the Hall was packed to bursting point

Dream Analysis: A psychological test. Each learner is required to find a partner to work with. They then take it in turns to ask each other a set of five questions that can be found on the worksheet. The interpretations are presented below and can be handed out once the learners have exchanged their answers.

1. The door represents the future. If it is open, it means you're positive about the future. If it's closed, then the future is something that frightens you.
2. The animal represents problems with people. If it is a large, wild and dangerous animal, then it is likely they are big ones. What you do to the animal reveals how good you are at coping with the problems you have.
3. The small shiny object represents how important money is to you. If you see something expensive and pick it up, then money is likely to be your main concern in life.
4. The wall represents a major crisis in your life. The bigger the wall is, the bigger you imagine your problem to be. If you walk around the wall or turn back, you're clearly struggling to

cope and perhaps you should consider seeking some kind of help.

5. The more water you see, the more important love is in your life. If you are in the water or you touch it, it means that you're in a relationship or that being in a relationship holds no fear for you.

THE DREAMS OF A KING

Once upon a time (perhaps it was yesterday or maybe even tomorrow) in a land far away (or maybe closer than you think) there lived a king who was plagued by a recurrent nightmare, of a fruit tree that would bear no fruit.

Despite his enormous wealth, as he had never learnt how to relate to people, the King was in fact an extremely lonely man. However, over the years he had learnt how to compensate for his discomfort with people by spending more and more time in his extensive gardens, which became so much of an obsession with the King that nothing else seemed to matter to him.

Not content with merely supervising the work on the land, the King went to great pains to ensure it was fully protected from any unwelcome intruders by surrounding the Palace grounds with all the latest security measures – ferocious guard dogs, high walls, fences of razor wire and 24-hour video surveillance – all with the purpose of ensuring his Garden of Eden was truly impenetrable. In view of the King's obsession, the consternation the recent spate of dreams had caused the monarch came as no surprise to those who knew him well.

Night after night, as soon as the King laid his royal head on the pillow and closed his eyes, the vision would return to haunt him and give him no peace. At his wits end, the sovereign turned to his advisors who summoned the leading medical experts from all over the land to examine him and diagnose the cause of his condition.

Their recommendations were as varied as their specialities, ranging from sleeping on a bed of nails to the application of blood-sucking leeches, from the King drinking three glasses of his own urine daily to a strict seven-day fast. Being a renowned gourmet, it was this last suggestion that displeased him the most and he responded by having the nutritionist who suggested it beheaded. Not surprisingly, the visits from the various specialists dried up after that.

In desperation, the King sent for his Head Gardener, a wise old soul who was never afraid to say what he thought regardless of whether it met with royal approval or not. As an expert on the folklore of trees, surely his trusted and loyal servant would be able to interpret the meaning of the dream and so put an end to his suffering.

When the Head Gardener heard the dream, his interpretation, to the King's surprise, was a positive one. "Sometimes the trees that do bear fruit only sustain those who are beyond salvation and who serve no useful purpose in any case. At least the tree in your dream cannot be misused in this way."

On hearing this, the King responded by asking to be left on his own as he wanted time to reflect on his trusted servant's strange interpretation, which left him even more puzzled than he had been before. It was a hot, sticky, summer afternoon and as he lay on the couch by the window overlooking the gardens, he soon drifted off to sleep.

As usual, he found himself standing in front of the fruit tree but this time it was dripping with fruit - exotic fruit of all shapes and sizes, the likes of which the King had never seen before. And the fruit tree was surrounded by all the King's courtiers who were gorging themselves on the succulent produce, stuffing themselves silly. Meanwhile, the poor people excluded from the Royal Gardens by the high railings, could only look on hungrily and watch the proceedings. As for the King, he had never noticed the crowds outside the railings before. In fact, he had become so engrossed in his garden over the years, to the detriment of everything else, that he'd forgotten they even existed.

The new dream, in a way, was even more disturbing than the previous one and left the King a chastened man. He immediately resolved to summon all his people to the Main Hall to deliver a speech. Nobody could remember the last time the King had shown any interest in addressing his subjects so the Hall was packed to bursting point for this extraordinary occasion.

" Never having had the opportunity to relate to my fellow human beings as an equal, I have always felt uncomfortable in the company of others and have devoted my life to caring for my vegetables and trees instead. And in my greed to protect what I falsely believed belonged to me, I did everything in my power to ensure that the fruit of my labour would be inaccessible to everyone else. But I know now that we will be provided for and that we should give thanks for what we will be given even before we receive it. For it is only by showing faith that our needs can be met. Instead of directing our energies to protecting what was never intended to belong to anyone in the first place, our time would be better spent in ensuring its equal distribution to all. So from this day on, I decree that the gates of the Palace will always be open, open to everyone whatever their status might be. And I have every confidence that rather than leading to any shortage, the result will be more than enough for everyone."

And from that day on, nobody in the Kingdom ever went short of food again. As for the King, by mingling among the visitors who came to the Garden, dressed inconspicuously in his overalls, he gradually learnt how to relate to people and began to enjoy life in a way that he had never imagined possible before. And the nightmares? They never returned.

THE DREAMS OF A KING: WORKSHEET

Find words in the story which mean the same as: a. tormented over and over again by the same bad dream b. In spite of his being incredibly rich c. make up for how ill-at-ease he felt d. made great efforts to be certain e. Completely at a loss as to what to do f. As he was well known for his interest in good food g. no matter whether the king agreed with him or not h. greedily eating as much as they could i. there was standing room only left in the Hall

By mingling among the visitors who came to the Garden, dressed inconspicuously in his overalls, he gradually learnt how to relate to people and began to enjoy life in a way that he had never imagined possible before. Notice how BY + ING can be used to answer the question HOW. Now complete the following sentence starters and endings in the same way:

1. By voting for the _____ Party in the next election, …
2. By recycling paper, plastic bottles, and cans, …
3. … you can help other people less fortunate than yourself.
4. By not only thinking of ourselves, …
5. By giving up smoking and drinking less alcohol, …
6. … we can help to make the world a better place.
7. By cycling to work instead of taking your car, …
8. By becoming a vegetarian, …
9. …you can learn how to manage your anger.
10. By treating others the same way we would like them to treat us, …
11. … we can ensure our children have a future.
12. By jogging through the park every morning, …

In small groups, work through the following questions, and then elect a spokesperson to present you answers to the rest of the class:

a. Do you suffer from insomnia or do you know anybody who does? What's supposed to be a good cure for the problem?
b. How often do you remember your dreams and how much importance do you attach to them?
c. Have you ever had a premonition in a dream that came true? Tell me about it.
d. Do you know anybody who talks or walks in their sleep? What are you supposed to do if you find someone walking in their sleep?
e. What do you know about interpreting the meaning of dreams?
f. Do you have any recurrent nightmares? If so, what are they about, and what do you think they signify?

Now for a psychological test to find out what your dreams mean. Find a partner to work with and take it in turns to ask each other the questions below:

1. Imagine you're dreaming and you see a door. Is it open or closed, locked or unlocked? Do you open it or do you do something else?

2. Next you see an animal. Which animal is it and what is it doing? Do you speak to it or do you do something else?

3. This time you see something small and shiny on the ground. What is it? Do you pick it up or do something else with it?

4. Next you come to a wall. What kind of wall is it and what do you? Do you try to climb over it, walk along it, or decide to go back where you came from?

5. Finally you see some water. What kind of water is it - a glass of water, a lake, a river or a sea? Do you touch the water or do you do something else?

When you have finished, exchange answers with someone else in the room and analyse what they have written for them based on the information your teacher will now give you:

BOOKS

O is a symbol of the world, of oneness and unity. In different cultures it also means the "eye," symbolizing knowledge and insight. We aim to publish books that are accessible, constructive and that challenge accepted opinion, both that of academia and the "moral majority."

Our books are available in all good English language bookstores worldwide. If you don't see the book on the shelves ask the bookstore to order it for you, quoting the ISBN number and title. Alternatively you can order online (all major online retail sites carry our titles) or contact the distributor in the relevant country, listed on the copyright page.

See our website www.o-books.net for a full list of over 500 titles, growing by 100 a year.

And tune in to myspiritradio.com for our book review radio show, hosted by June-Elleni Laine, where you can listen to the authors discussing their books.

MySpiritRadio